Journeys on the Edge

Burma – in a country in chaos, where nothing is as it appears to be, we undertake our personal quests.

Bob Anderson

Matador
Unit E2 Airfield Business Park,
Harrison Road, Market Harborough,
Leicestershire. LE16 7UL
Tel: 0116 279 2299
Email: books@troubador.co.uk
Web: www.troubador.co.uk/matador
Twitter: @matadorbooks

ISBN 978 1803135 021

British Library Cataloguing in Publication Data.
A catalogue record for this book is available from the British Library.

Printed and bound in Great Britain by 4edge Limited
Typeset in 11pt Minion by Troubador Publishing Ltd, Leicester, UK

Matador is an imprint of Troubador Publishing Ltd

To Jan, my darling wife, for her tolerance and forbearance and for her invaluable encouragement.

The staff and volunteers of MEP from Britain, Burma, Thailand and from that wider international community who share a common spirit and who, over the years, have built this organisation.

The Burmese people with whom we have worked, the Burman, Kachin, Karen, Mon whose kindness, dignity and resilience in such difficult circumstances impressed us, encouraged us and touched our hearts.

'It is in equal parts thrilling and affecting, but it is often laugh-out-loud funny too.'

— Will Millard BBC presenter, writer, and Patron of MEP

Introduction

On 1 February 2021 tanks appeared on the streets of Burmese cities, and as I write this introduction the people of Burma are involved in a seemingly endless struggle for justice and democracy.

This story traces the long path and the endeavours to build from scratch what was to become an award-winning charity. Mobile Education Partnerships works in communities displaced by war, poverty and oppression inside Burma (aka Myanmar) and on the Thai–Burmese border. This book invites you to share this journey, enter its chaotic, dangerous but fascinating world, and encounter its physical, emotional and spiritual challenges and dilemmas. However, this is not a sentimental presentation of 'victimhood' but a very candid, sympathetic and at times humorous exploration of how an organisation was built in these difficult circumstances. Neither is it a handbook on how to build a charity, but it does offer a ground-level guide to anyone who wishes to go down that road. I hope it also provides a compelling insight into Burma's tragic and at times bizarre social and political backdrop, drawing on the lives and journeys, both physical and spiritual, of those living on the edge, the refugees, the migrants, the warlords and the lost souls, many of whom are looking for something to believe in, and who are caught in a world in which nothing is as it appears to be.

Foreword

Will Millard

I initially spoke to Bob Anderson, founder of the award-winning charity Mobile Education Partnerships (MEP), at the turn of 2019. It was shortly after my series *My Year With The Tribe* had first aired on BBC Two, and, having seen my work in remote parts of the Asia Pacific, Bob recognised our shared passion for championing the rights of minority groups, and reached out to ask if I might be interested in becoming a patron of MEP.

To say I was honoured would be a massive understatement; but, as I have come to know the full extent of this charity's work, their extraordinary origins, and their incredibly committed staff, that sense of honour has only grown. I feel very privileged to know Bob and the people working at the core of the charity, and am very proud to have even a small association with their work.

As a writer and BBC broadcaster, so much of my job is spent reporting on disaffected, disenfranchised, forgotten or ignored peoples or places. We aim to raise awareness of an issue in a television programme, radio broadcast, or piece of writing, before inevitably we have to move on to the next. You hope, as you go, that you might make something of a credible difference by bringing an issue to mainstream attention, but that is a world apart from actually creating the mechanisms for long-term change.

Bob, alongside a dedicated band of colleagues, educational specialists, and teachers from right across Britain and Myanmar, have built MEP from the ground up. For over two decades, through warfare, the recent coronavirus pandemic, and all of the collective challenges of working within such a remote and logistically challenging place, the resolve of MEP has never once wavered.

MEP's mobile units of teacher trainers have reached scattered and displaced communities throughout Myanmar and its international borders. They have brought quality education to some of the most vulnerable refugee communities and ethnic minorities on the Asian continent. They have trained thousands of local teachers, providing them with resources and clearing the pathway for them to receive professional accreditations; changing the direction of tens of thousands of their student children in the process.

The power of education in changing people's lives for the better cannot possibly be overstated. Without basic literacy and numeracy skills, children are far more likely to spend their lifetime in poverty, and are much more at risk from exploitation and trafficking; but, in an all-too frequently war-torn nation, education can also provide the tools, the confidence and self-belief, to create credible pathways towards peace.

This book is the warts-and-all, and, at times, devastatingly honest, account of how it is possible to triumph against seemingly insurmountable odds. It is the story of how one small charity has made one huge difference, and is one almighty adventure into this most-misunderstood corner of Southeast Asia. It is in equal parts thrilling and affecting, but it is often laugh-out-loud funny too. In Bob, the reader has one of life's truly great storytellers as their guide to the Republic of Myanmar, its history, its hidden peoples, and their fascinating cultures. It is a joy to read and inspires throughout.

Having got to know Bob and his brilliance, I fully expected Journeys on the Edge to be as wonderfully told as it is, but this is also a deeply moving account with a very powerful message at its core: even in the very darkest of places, hope will prevail for as long as we hold on to our common humanity, our courage, and, above all, our kindness.

Will Millard.
BBC presenter, writer, and Patron of MEP.

Notes on Structure

The chapters, in general, are ordered chronologically and follow the development of Mobile Education Partnerships.

This covers a period of over twenty years so in order to maintain the pace of the narrative I had to summarise activities which took place over a number of years. The summaries are to be found in the occasional 'Moving On' sections, which appear between some of the main chapters.

Inevitably the situation has thrown up dozens of acronyms. I've included a list in the Appendix.

There may be some readers who might wish to build their own small organisations and in the 'Taking Stock' sections I've added summaries of my own experience, which I hope may prove useful to those wishing to go down this road.

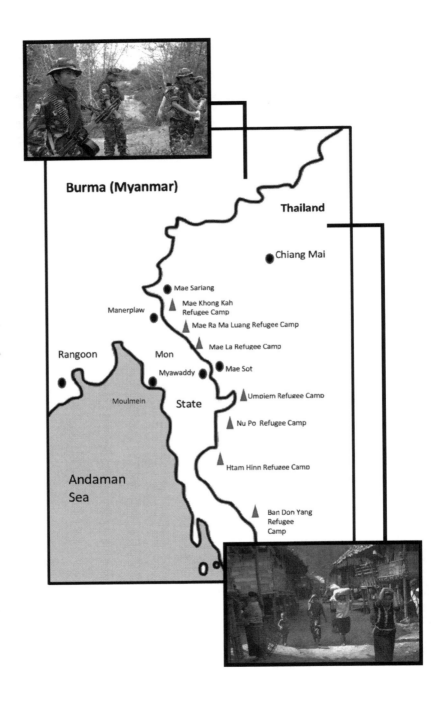

Burma (Myanmar)

Thailand

Chiang Mai

Mae Sariang

Mae Khong Kah
Refugee Camp

Manerplaw

Mae Ra Ma Luang Refugee Camp

Mae La Refugee Camp

Rangoon

Mon

Myawaddy

Mae Sot

Moulmein

State

Umpiem Refugee Camp

Nu Po Refugee Camp

Andaman
Sea

Htam Hinn Refugee Camp

Ban Don Yang
Refugee
Camp

Historical Context

Burma, or Myanmar as it is now called, is a country inhabited by eight major ethnic groups, each with its own language, culture and history. The dominant group are the Bama or Burmans. They and the other groups – the Karen, Kachin, Mon et al. – all come under the more generic heading of 'Burmese', as does the central government. The problem is that the Burmans tend to dominate the political and military establishment and form the military government, which has been running Burma for nearly sixty years. During this period the smaller ethnic groups have been fighting for a level of autonomy against this military government.

In the eighteenth century, Burma was a major power in Southeast Asia. Through a series of wars, it expanded its territory into what is now northern Thailand and then into the Arakan, which bordered Bengal, at that time under the control of the British East India Company. In 1824 a border conflict involving refugees fleeing from the Arakan triggered a war with the British. By 1885, following two further wars, Burma became a British colony. Its king was exiled to India and the feudal system dismantled. Burma was ruled from Calcutta by the Raj. During the colonial period the Burmans were excluded from the army while the British favoured the smaller ethnic groups often known as the Hill Peoples, such as the Karen and the Kachin. A significant split occurred during World War II when the Burmans, under General Aung San, sided with the Japanese while the Hill Peoples supported the British.

Independence came in 1948 and, as the country's first president, Aung San moved towards the construction of a federal state. He was assassinated in the same year. The country fell into civil war, and after ten years the fledgling and rather beleaguered democracy began to move towards the establishment of a federal union. A military coup in 1962 ended that process, and a lengthy civil conflict began.

Prologue

The Herdsman

Hett, Durham, England, 29 April 2020

In a Zen Buddhist text known as *Gentling the Bull* a character referred to is called the herdsman. The herdsman is a personification of an aspiration. An aspiration, we all feel, that something is missing that we need to find, which is termed 'the bull'. The herdsman does not know exactly what the bull looks like or where to find the elusive creature, and his search is long and difficult. The quest is essentially a spiritual quest, the quest for wholeness on which we all embark. It has much rough ground as the herdsman discovers that to which he is most attached is not the true path. We look for our Grail in the material or spiritual world when its location is not to be found in one thing either mental or physical but in all things.

In our midriff we feel there is a gaping hole, the source
of our insecurity, of our aggression, and our wants, of
blunders and of fears.
(*Gentling the Bull* by Ven. Myokyo-ni)

Over twenty thousand of us in Britain have died so far in the coronavirus pandemic. The reality of it all became even more personal last week when a letter from HM Government arrived informing me that I am 'at risk' and should practise social distancing inside my home. I am to be 'shielded'. This is an uncomfortable prospect, but I have no wish to add to the statistics. As if to confirm my isolation, a food parcel arrived this morning followed by a phone call from Sharron at Wellbeing for Life checking on the vulnerable! I can't believe that at seventy-one I am now vulnerable when I had hoped to be at least approaching venerable.

However, whatever the grim reality of the present, I cannot distance myself from the past. A small metal figure stares at me from the top of my desk. It sits relaxed on a lotus, head turned towards me, thumb and forefinger of each hand in a mudra, almost ready to spring to life and clash the two tiny cymbals on its feet. This is the Law Ka Nat, the Burmese incarnation of the *boddhisattva* of compassion, also known as Avalokiteshvara, as Kwan Yin and as Kannon; the 'one who hears the cries of the world'. Its sublime smile invites my own smile, and the past, as a continuous karmic stream of life, flows into the present.

One

The Rabbit Hole

Refugees, Rebels and Agatha Christie, Mae Sariang, Thai–Burmese Border, April 1996

"It's no use going back to yesterday,
because I was a different person then."
(*Alice's Adventures in Wonderland* by Lewis Carroll)

"Is there anything you need, sir?" The words, softly spoken, floated out of the darkness, inviting an answer which could be practical or deeply philosophical. In the immediate context my answer was simple – a glass of water to wash down bitter antimalarial pills – but the question's full implications took me another twenty years, and another life, to answer. This quest required the swallowing of many more bitter pills, but was sweetened by so much that was good.

The night was stiflingly hot in Mae Sariang. The buildings – of concrete, corrugated iron and bamboo –

gave the town a rather ramshackle charm, but from here led dusty roads and winding tracks through the jungles of the Dawna Range to the porous border between Thailand and Burma. This was the territory of drug traffickers, warlords and, most recently, refugees from the Karen ethnic group. It was also my intended destination.

I was a teacher by profession, working in East Durham, one of the most deprived areas in Britain, but when time allowed I freelanced as a photographer for the London agency Rex Features. Over the years this had taken me to some of the most volatile parts of the world during crucial times in their history. I had been in Nicaragua when the revolutionary Sandinista government defended itself against the US-backed Contras, in the Philippines during the communist insurgency following the fall of Ferdinand Marcos, in the Cambodian refugee camps on the Thai border following the defeat of the Khmer Rouge, and in Cambodia itself for its first elections. History had drawn me to these places as it now drew me towards Burma.

Fighting had broken out all along the Thai–Burmese border between ethnic Karen insurgents and the Burmese army, the Tatmadaw, resulting in thousands of Karen villagers fleeing to Thailand for safety. Two days previously in Mae Sot I had been stuck at a roadblock manned by the black-clad Thai border force. An edgy young soldier with an M16 rifle had shaken his head at my requests to continue along the border road. Burmese armed groups had crossed the border further north and were demanding money from travellers. The Thai army had sealed the border and closed roads along a hundred-mile stretch that I had intended to travel in order to get to Mae Sariang and from there into the Karen camps. The Thais had blocked the road, so, after a day's journey along a circuitous route away from the border, I arrived in Mae Sariang – but how then to get into the camps? The whole area was off limits and Bon, my Thai guide, who ran a small travel company, was worried. Temples and elephants for tourists was his business and this was beyond his remit. He wouldn't go any further, and failure looked inevitable.

The rooms in the small hotel were airless. Opening the tap into the washbasin only resulted in a dribble of water and a metallic groan from the depths of the pipe. There was no bottled water, and lubrication was needed if the required antimalarial tablets were to be taken. I wandered out into the darkness of the corridor, hoping for some solution. That's when I heard the voice asking if I needed anything. Out of the gloom stepped what appeared to be a youngish man in T-shirt and shorts. He disappeared into the night and quickly returned with a can of Coca-Cola. I had assumed he was Thai, but as he stretched out his arm in the half-light I noticed it was tattooed. This is common in the area in question, but what was remarkable about this tattoo was that it comprised a clutch of crudely inked words in English: 'God is Love'. A few years later I saw the same tattoo on the stump of an arm blown off by a landmine, reminding us, perhaps, of the limits of divine protection. The young man introduced himself as Truelove. He was a Karen refugee and quickly offered to be my guide to the camps.

Unless totally deluded, you would rightly conclude that a brief meeting in a darkened corridor with a complete stranger is not a sound basis for making an informed decision, especially one involving potential encounters with armed insurgents. A check was needed. Truelove was a porter at the hotel but also a general handyman at the nearby Catholic church. I decided an early morning visit to the priest would help me determine my course of action. The Father, a grey-bearded Italian, was rather taken aback by my unexpected visit but explained that Truelove was indeed who he said he was and that I could trust him. Truelove had an 'uncle' with a pickup truck, and a price was arranged.

Early the following morning, in a dramatic rush of dust and grinding gears, a blue truck arrived containing Truelove and three cheerful 'uncles', all with wide grins displaying red, betel-stained teeth. The truck looked serviceable enough. Bon had abandoned his tour-guide role and any hopes of quietly surveying the local temples and was now up for the trip, and joined me on the wooden plank placed across the truck's open back.

One likes to travel hopefully and despite a certain nervousness our spirits were up as we passed a major, and comforting, landmark. There are many large Buddhas in Thailand but outside Mae Sariang sits a massive Buddha figure which is all the more impressive as it is completely white. It dominates the countryside for miles, serenely overlooking the neat, green rice paddies that eventually give way to low, scrub-covered hills, and in the distance are the blue mountains of the Burmese border and all of the secrets they contain. The truck followed a sealed road for about a mile and then turned off onto a dirt track, churning up clouds of red dust. The dust stifled any attempts at conversation, and despite our efforts to take shelter behind the cab, the ride threatened to be long and hard. Over the next few miles I lost track of the time, but suddenly the truck slowed and began to turn off the dirt road. This seemed odd as there was no other discernible track to take. It quickly became obvious what was happening. Gradually, the 'uncle' driving eased the truck over a bank onto a dried-up riverbed strewn with rocks. This was the way into the mountains and the entrance to the 'rabbit hole'. Reaching our destination now seemed a possibility, in spite of the sharp rocks that littered the riverbed.

The truck lurched from side to side, trying to avoid damage to its undercarriage as we made our way further into the hills. The bush grew dense on the riverbanks, but suddenly within a clearing there appeared a bamboo hut. A group of men piled out of the hut and blocked our path. Although dressed in sarongs and shirts, they were from the Thai border guard, and they were drunk. Let me assure you from uncomfortable personal experience that drunken soldiers are at best unpredictable and at worst downright dangerous. Even the 'uncles' were rather fazed as an officer in a hula shirt and a checked sarong asked for my passport. He thumbed through the document, then, with very deliberate actions, began to write my name on his 'pad', which on closer inspection turned out to be a copy of *Playboy* magazine. My name was added to the front cover alongside 'Bunny of the Month'. The 'uncles' were now all betel-red smiles, and the squaddies giggled drunkenly. Minor humiliation over and potential trouble avoided, we lurched on further down the rabbit hole.

Stands of bamboo covered the riverbanks. It's such an elegant plant, and with stems thirty feet high and thicker than a man's leg it formed a shady tunnel. We moved on, painstakingly avoiding the rocks in the dappled light, and on easing round a bend in the river our path was again blocked by a man in a red sarong, naked to the waist, heavily tattooed and carrying a large knife. He was obviously as surprised as we were, and called out into the bamboo. Like an echo the call was repeated along the length of the tunnel as other tattooed men appeared from the tall stands, all carrying knives. We stared at one another for a moment, and then Truelove grinned happily, the 'uncles' were radiant, and gradually the surprise on the faces of the tattooed men turned to smiles and they waved us through. We had found the Karen.

From the bank on our left, stretching up into the hills, straggled a village of bamboo huts, all on stilts. Out of one ran a man in a khaki military shirt and a red sarong. Holding up a large book with a cross crudely imprinted on the cover, he said in good English, "Welcome to Mae Khong Kah camp." He was at pains for us to see the book, which contained handwritten lists of names all neatly recorded in what was obviously some form of antique ledger. "These are the names of all of the people in the camp," he announced quite proudly. Mae Khong Kah, named after the Thai goddess of water, turned out to be one of the Karen camps hastily erected along the border.

Bon, Truelove and the 'uncles' stayed with the truck while I was ushered up the bank and then a ladder into a very large, airy hut with what appeared to be a shrine on one wall. This turned out to be Christian, with a gilt crucifix in front of a poster painting of the bearded Christ, eyes turned upwards. Golden objects on a red cloth covered the rest of the table. A man of middle years appeared, slight but confident in manner, with sharp, mobile eyes. He introduced himself as Paul, the camp leader and a Catholic. In excellent English he explained that the villagers had fled from fighting in the Papun area and more were coming across the border on a daily basis and had to be accommodated. At this time I had little knowledge of the roots of the Karen's struggle, or the Karen themselves. That would come with time. Their main concern in 1996 was not actually the Burmese army but an offshoot of their own forces known as the Democratic Karen Buddhist Army (DKBA), which had transferred its loyalties to the junta. Essentially, the Karen were fighting for an autonomous state, which they called Kawthoolei ('Land of Flowers' seems to be one rough translation). Led by General Bo Mya, a former British soldier and now head of the Karen National Union (KNU), they had established their capital in the village of Manerplaw. In January 1995 Manerplaw had fallen to the Burmese army and thousands of Karen had fled to Thailand for safety.

Paul and I ascended a dusty path, which straggled alongside a stream that ran through the village. The houses were neatly constructed of split bamboo and pandanus leaf, with the main living area forming a platform supported by sturdy hardwood piles. Chickens and pigs lived underneath the platform, picking up scraps that dropped through the slats. The chickens, some scrawny and suffering from some kind of foul pest exposing areas of skin, then became dinner. It looked to be a well-integrated cycle. Further structures had been built onto many houses in what seemed like afterthoughts. They looked, and were, precarious. A young lady in a flowered sarong stooped by the stream, ladling water into half a dozen plastic jerrycans, while three children lined up for my photocall. The smell of woodsmoke floated on the light breeze as we worked our way up the hillside towards the upper village, which bordered stands of what my English eye perceived as a tropical version of silver birch. Some houses had fish ponds, a habitat for the local bony favourite, catfish, and red-faced Muscovy ducks which splashed around the edges. Wood seemed to be at the heart of everything. Along with the smoke, its general aroma scented the air. A group of women – grandmother in a red turban, two daughters in dark sarongs and with babies in slings around their shoulders – sat on logs at the edge of the path beside a huge plant laden with small white flowers. They looked to be resting after hauling loads in bamboo baskets on their backs with the weight taken by a forehead band. All smiled that gentle Karen smile that sits in front of dark, curious eyes, and which I came to know so well. The baking silence of an early afternoon in the tropics was broken by a rhythmic creak and thud as two teenage girls operated a kind of 'hobby horse' contraption with a heavy head which thumped into a large wooden bowl containing raw rice. One girl depressed the tail of the horse with her foot, while the other had the much more dangerous job of pushing the rice under the head. This all required a level of coordination and much trust, but they jumped and laughed as they made light of their rice-husking task. This did not seem like the classic refugee camp of blue tarpaulins, mud and fear, but a Karen community, intact and functioning in what could easily be taken for a rural idyll. However, reality was soon to suggest otherwise.

Paul and I continued our ascent. Now and again, he

would halt to readjust his *teku*[1] and complain about his difficulty in keeping up with people with long legs. 'Long Legs' proved to be a name of historical significance to the Karen. It was part of the British connection that became more and more apparent, important and, sadly, bitter as I got to know them. During World War II Karen levies had been raised by British officers to fight a guerrilla campaign after the British army had been forced out of Burma by the invading Japanese in 1942. British officers had been parachuted into Karen territory and successfully set up Force 136, made up of Karen recruits. One of the most well respected of these officers was Hugh Seagrim, a young man of six feet, four inches in height. The Karen nicknamed him Hpu Taw Kaw, or Grandfather Long Legs. 'Grandfather' would never go down too well in the West, but amongst the Burmese it is a title which indicates much respect. Seagrim certainly earned the Karen's respect, leading them in guerrilla operations against the Japanese (with, according to one source, a Bible under one arm and a Tommy gun under the other), and when the Japanese forces threatened a *tobatsu* – the burning of Karen villagers and summary executions – should they fail to hand over the Englishman, Seagrim, accompanied by seven Karen, handed himself in. All were executed. However, attitudes towards the British had another, darker aspect which I would learn about later.

Paul was worried about the influx of refugees into the camp, but he had graver concerns on his mind. Now that they were on the Thai side of the border, their safety was not guaranteed. On 3 May 1995 the Burmese had sent

---

1   A man's sarong.

detachments of their new allies, the DKBA, to attack the camps. Three Thai policemen had been killed in a gunfight with thirty to forty uniformed Burmese who'd poured across the border to attack a Karen refugee camp. The camp was abandoned after the attackers burned down more than a hundred bamboo huts used by the refugees. Thailand responded by sending helicopter gunships across the border to attack a village described as a headquarters for the Burmese rebels. According to news reports in Bangkok, the attack destroyed a Buddhist monastery and killed fifteen villagers. An Amnesty report from 1 June 1995 echoed the concerns of Paul and many others in the camp. It cited the words of a thirty-eight-year-old unmarried woman from Mae Ta Waw camp:

"We have no place to go, no place to hide... What will I do if the DKBA come again? If they burn my house, then I'll build a small house in its place. If they take us, we won't go. If they shoot us, we'll have to die... Everyone is troubled, depressed. But our whole lives have been full of problems, so problems are not strange to us."

She had been forced to flee her village in Hpa-an district after her house had been twice destroyed, four of her friends killed, and the Tatmadaw commander had ordered her to sleep with him on pain of death. Over the coming years these stories became commonplace to me, reflecting those told by Karen volunteers who worked for us, and who became our teachers, trainers and friends. As a result, Mae Khong Kah was under constant guard. Night patrols protected the perimeter, and a warning system was set up. Bamboo poles with watchtowers ran through the camps, and every hour the stillness of the night was broken by the *tok-tok* of bamboo on bamboo as sentries beat the poles to indicate that all was safe in their section. One of the problems Paul faced was that the attackers were likely to be fellow Karen from the newly formed DKBA. This made distinguishing friend from foe something of a difficulty, and what he feared most was spies. He told me, "They could enter our camp easily. I worry one day someone will throw a hand grenade into my house." This fear, and his responsibility as camp leader, weighed heavily on Paul, and a few months later it coloured his judgement. Two strangers *did* enter the camp and were arrested by the guard. Paul had to make a life-or-death decision. Other camps had been attacked and fear was everywhere. He had the two men executed. Later it turned out that they had not been spies, and Paul was questioned by the KNU leadership but did not face punishment. I saw him a year later, a silent and withdrawn man. With his comment on my first day in Mae Khong Kah the rural idyll vanished like a child's dream.

As we continued our climb the conversation turned to politics. This was 1996 and the new millennium was in sight. I found it difficult to believe that the fighting was still going on, and mentioned that surely the internationally famous icon of democracy Aung San Suu Kyi held out some hope for the future. This comment was met with nothing short of controlled disdain from Paul. "What can she do?" It was not a comment that hinted at the difficulties of Aung San Suu Kyi being under house arrest, but smacked of something deeper, something much more visceral. Paul held no hopes for her doing anything much to help the Karen. I found later that this was a deeply held view which, like everything in this conundrum, had its roots in the gloom of Burmese history.

The British generally get the blame for much in Burma but it often depends on with whom you are talking. Opinions tend to be split along ethnic lines and are often rooted in the nature of Burma's link with the British. Prior to British rule, Burma, under its last native dynasty, the Konbaung, had a kind of loose suzerainty over its border areas, the Shan, Chin, Kachin, Karenni and Karen. These are the ethnic groups known to the Burman majority as the Dain Yin Thar and to the former British colonial administration as the Hill Peoples. They are not part of the dominant Burman group which ruled the country for hundreds of years. On taking over the country following three wars ending in 1885, the British cultivated strong links with the Dain Yin Thar including the Karen, who were, according to some sources, not strictly one of the Hill Peoples as many Karen lived in lowland Burma but, importantly, they were not Burman either. In general, the British ruled the border areas with a light touch, allowing local rulers to maintain their power, with a little British 'advice'. The Burman majority were not treated in the same way. The British exiled their last king, Thibaw, and brought to an end the feudal system and all of the inherited privileges and class and economic structures it supported. They even excluded the Burmans from joining the newly formed army. This really rankled as the British set up Karen and Kachin rifle regiments and the Chin fought in the British army in Mesopotamia in World War I. In late 1941 the Burmans saw their chance when the Japanese invasion chased the British back to India. Bogyoke[2] Aung San (Aung San Suu Kyi's father), having spearheaded the independence movement for some years and received military training from the Japanese, raised Burman regiments to join the fight against the British. And here lay one root of the current problem: the Karen and Kachin fought as guerrillas for the British alongside officers such as Hugh Seagrim. The result was an ugly civil war with Burman attacks on Karen villages and terrible atrocities committed. Aung San and the rest of Burma soon became disillusioned with Japanese rule, and when the British seemed to be winning Aung San changed sides – a sensible move; he was definitely a pragmatist. And when I look at the situation in Burma in 2020 I see something of that pragmatism in his daughter as, at that time de facto leader of the country, she trod carefully through the minefield of Burmese politics.

Paul pointed out a bamboo structure with a cross, which, he explained, was the Baptist church. About twenty-five per cent of the Karen were, seemingly, Christians and the rest mainly Buddhist. Much of the leadership was Christian, which many thought added to the friction leading to the recent split. A short distance away was an extensive building with rows of fixed bamboo 'desks' and long benches. This was the Baptist school. The head teacher's house was nearby, and, within a few moments, we were invited to climb into the home of Saw Htoo Wah, a man of middle years growing comfortably portly. The room was airy and open in the Karen style, and on one wall a hanging proclaimed 'Jesus

---

2   General.

Christ is head of this house'. On another a poster portrait of a youngish man with a long beard, more Castro than Christ, peered down sternly on proceedings. At that time, I had no idea how important this man was to the Karen. Saw Htoo Wah and his wife Naw Paw Reh spoke excellent English and produced tea poured through a tea strainer. They had fled the fighting near Papun and walked three days to the camp with their three children. I wondered why, in those pressing circumstances, it had been a priority to bring a tea strainer. That decision somehow held a deeper significance linked to home and civility. There was so much in this new world that conjured up the ghosts of Empire and links with the British. The fact that I was English prompted serious questioning from Naw Paw Reh about the state of the monarchy, and especially Prince Charles and his wife Diana. "Who is to blame for their separation?" she asked quite pointedly. Not being abreast of royal scandals, I couldn't offer much of an opinion, which was rather disappointing for Naw Paw Reh as she had clearly taken Diana's side. In my situation at that time, exchanges such as this seemed almost surreal but strangely comforting and rather quaint. In a subsequent conversation with Saw Htoo Wah the Karen's bittersweet relationship with the British became even more evident, and a theme which was to pervade the next twenty-five years of my relationship with the Karen began to take shape. The story goes something like this.

The Karen had been loyal to the British during World War II, but that loyalty had been cultivated by the promise of one thing that was really important to them: independence. They had long wished to throw off the yoke of the Burmans and had seen the British as a means by which to achieve this when British officers promised them an independent state if they cooperated in driving out the Japanese and reinstating British rule. This they did, but the post-war British government under Clement Attlee had enough on its plate with the partition of India and decided to back a central government under Aung San, a Burman. Karen requests for independence were refused and a deep sense of betrayal and resentment began to fester. Following British withdrawal from Burma in 1948, civil war ensued, with the Karen led by a Cambridge-trained lawyer, Saw Ba U Gyi; the bearded young man whose picture hung above me. He'd gained martyr status after his assassination in 1950, two years after Aung San suffered the same fate. Following about ten years of fragile democracy, a military government took control of a country riven by ethnic and communist insurgencies. An offensive was launched against the Karen. Operating under the rather graphic title of The Four Cuts (essentially, 'Cut them off from their recruits, intelligence, supplies and funding'), it led to 140,000 refugees pouring over the border into Thailand. The Karen told me darkly that the fifth cut was 'Cut off their heads'. Many Western activists saw the whole operation as genocide. The military government, now known internationally by the rather Orwellian title of the State Law and Order Restoration Council (SLORC), backed a centralised union, while the Karen and other ethnic groups wanted various levels of autonomy and regarded the union as an attempt by the dominant Burman group to run things their way both politically and culturally. Both sides had their icons, their myths and their prejudices, which had sustained them through almost half a century of civil war.

Before I left I offered to support the Karen if possible. Saw Htoo Wah turned this over briefly and asked if I could find teachers for the camp schools. This was a tall order, but I said I would look into it. His wife had a request too. Conversations with the Karen are frequently punctuated by pregnant, thoughtful silences, lubricated by much chewing of betel nut. This was one such moment. Naw Paw Reh looked up and, with the deep conviction of a recent convert, said, "Could you please bring me some Agatha Christie novels?" There was a poignancy in this simple request. Righting wrongs comforts all humans, whether in the Cotswolds or deep in the Dawna Range. The moral balance of the cosmos is restored. However, the Karen needed more than Hercule Poirot to sort out this human tragedy. It was time to leave the rabbit hole. I would return with the books, and, in time, the teachers would come too.

Two

Among the Axe Handles

Paranoid Generals, a Very Serious Man, and The Lady, Yangon (Rangoon), April 1996

Yangon airport was dusty confusion. Soldiers were everywhere, all armed with automatic weapons and big smiles. The junta was putting on a show. The SLORC had proudly displayed its new-found liberalism by designating 1996 as 'The Year of the Tourist'. Burma was marketed as an exotic, unspoilt destination with friendly, smiling people. Obviously, the soldiers at the airport liked their new image. This was a year when visas were extended and travel within the country opened up just a little with the aim of attracting half a million tourists. There seemed to be something of an imbalance here, as a 1995 report by the International Trade Union Confederation had pointed out that one million inhabitants of Burma were expelled from their dwellings to make way for those tourists. This was a million miles away from the refugee camps of the Thai border which I had just left, but we now had internal displacement. Aung San Suu Kyi, the great hope for democracy who had been so dismissed by the Karen, was under house arrest and had encouraged tourists not to visit Myanmar. The junta had labelled her an 'axe handle', a quaint but menacing expression referring to an insider who damages the status quo; the axe handle being made of the same wood as the tree it assaults. Undoubtedly, some of my money would go to keeping some rather unpleasant people in a style to which they had become accustomed, some would go to the small travel company I was using, and hopefully I could get some sense of the real state of the country in photos and words that might be syndicated through Rex. But how to get to any of this? Photojournalists of a political persuasion were definitely personae non gratae and possibly 'assistant axe handles'.

The first junta scam emerged at the airport. Big signs in English instructed tourists to exchange $300 (at the government rate) at the designated desk before leaving the building. The junta was partial to signs, as I was to find out. Ignoring the instruction, I had my paperwork completed in triplicate, I believe, and pushed through the crowds, soldiers and stifling heat to emerge into the light, where, amongst the taxi drivers touting for business, stood a youngish, solidly built man in a checked shirt and jeans, thankfully carrying a piece of cardboard bearing my name. He introduced himself as Mo. In the car, driving to the hotel, he quietly asked what my intentions were in Burma. This is where things inevitably start to become tense. At once I was back in the darkened hallway in Mae Sariang with the voice whispering, "Is there anything you need, sir?" I wanted to get a sense of the country and what was happening politically but, at that point, there was no way I was prepared to mention that to Mo. I stumbled through a couple of sentences about a trip up to Shan State that I had planned; part of the limited tourist route that was developing at that time. Mo was having none of this. The photographer's jacket and khaki camera bag were a giveaway. "You are here to see The Lady," he said with a weighty finality. It was a fixed conclusion, not an enquiry. This was no invitation to some sleazy bar, but obviously a reference to Aung San Suu Kyi. The moment that faces all travellers to Burma had arrived: to trust or not to trust? Here might be a chance – or would it lead to 'difficulties'? I had been told to be careful; informers were everywhere. My clumsy attempts to feign ignorance of the identity of 'The Lady' sounded hollow to Mo even in a second language. Perhaps he was, in fact, an axe handle! And so you give yourself, with much anxiety, into the charge of strangers, hoping that things will somehow work out. Mo was serious. Serious about The Lady. Serious about my trip. He viewed my offer of a beer at the hotel as almost a capital offence, and in the bar surveyed the well-heeled Burmese in their suits, uniforms and *longyis* with a hard-edged disgust. An itinerary – Mo's very serious itinerary – was agreed. He was earnest in his planning. Shan State was an irrelevance, he thought; he would change my flight. Firstly, a 'tour' of Yangon was scheduled, but dreamy golden pagodas were not on the menu; harsh reality was. This was serious business. And so it began.

Early the next morning Mo arrived looking more earnest than ever and ground rules were established.

And really here is the problem that faces anyone on a photojournalistic project such as this: you may get caught; you may be detained for a while and your film confiscated; you may be put on the next flight back to Bangkok, but that's it – you will be on that flight. The Mos of this world are not going anywhere, and therefore you have a responsibility when someone goes out of their way for you at some risk. So, Mo had rules. In the street, at meaningful locations of his choice, he would stop the car. I could take photos from the window and sometimes get out for a closer look. Mo would not walk with me, but remain at a distance.

First stop was the Swe Taw Myat Pagoda, then under construction by the SLORC. It was claimed that it would contain a tooth of the Buddha donated by the Chinese government. Relations with the Chinese were very important to the SLORC and vice versa, with the Chinese seeing Burma as part of their longer-term regional strategic plan. Spiritual matters were also important. Crucially, the SLORC was very interested in keeping on the right side of the Buddhist monks, the Sangha, and the junta leaders were generally held to be a superstitious lot, often with beliefs that fell well out of the Theravada Buddhism, which constituted the faith of the general populace. General Ne Win, who had led the military takeover in 1962 and remained in power until 1988, was reputed to be particularly superstitious. Although he had now 'retired' it was felt that he still had significant clout. He seems to have been influenced by numerology, and considered nine his lucky number. Hence, in 1987, according to some sources, he withdrew the 50- and 100-kyat notes and replaced them with denominations of 45 and 90; both divisible by nine.

This led to the ruin of many people who had their savings in the old denominations. Having said that, the opposition to Ne Win, notably the students, also had a superstitious bent. The big uprising against the military was held on 8 August 1988: 8/8/88. Even the undergraduate population were amateur numerologists.

The junta needed more than lucky numbers. In Burma many observers say that leadership creates a certain paranoia in those at the top. This prompts them to use increasingly heavy-handed measures, and hence increases resentment. It's a downward spiral. A creeping paranoia may have been the reason for the SLORC's need for endorsement from a higher source: the revered Buddhist Sangha itself. Also, in Theravada Buddhism one can make up for past misdeeds and create good *vipaka* (the results of one's karmic actions) by making merit (*punna*). Generosity and living by a moral code are all part of this, but a kind of 'edifice complex' had crept in whereby it was widely held that erecting a stupa might eradicate the results of bad karmic actions. In medieval Europe knights involved in what we would now call war crimes paid priests to pray for their souls, so avoiding, they believed, the dark consequences of their actions. The SLORC were obviously hoping for the same outcome.

Whatever the reason behind the progress, the Swe Taw Myat Pagoda was definitely under way. And what's more, it had nine entrances! As Mo pointed out with some gravity, this was not usual but, in fact, the SLORC playing the numbers game. The first storey of the pagoda grew from the white base and its spire poked through a mesh of bamboo scaffolding. A digger sat idly next to a row of bamboo huts draped with washing. Suddenly, a truck clattered into the building site, stirring up a cloud of red dust. A troop of men in dusty camouflage uniforms alighted and one raised a red, blue and yellow tricolour with a large white five-pointed star: the flag of the Burmese police. Following the flagbearer, the men marched in line towards the pagoda. From another direction, a file of what appeared to be civilians wearing blue jackets strode towards the pagoda steps. Mo explained the situation. The labour was supposed to be voluntary but in fact it was obligatory, or near enough, for government workers, of whom many would be members of the government-created workers' organisation known as the Union Solidarity and Development Association (USDA). It looked like a military operation and I found out later that, in fact, it was. The government newspaper *The New Light of Myanmar*, in an article published on 3 April, stated that officers, NCOs and Tatamadawmen (Air), led by Lieutenant Colonel Win Oo and ninety devotees, were helping to build the tooth relic pagoda. The police didn't get a mention; maybe they were mucking in as the 'devotees'.

Clearly, the junta was having a pagoda fest. Pagodas and various holy relics, mainly teeth, were everywhere in the news. That week, several stories in *The New Light of Myanmar* ran alongside pictures showing men in uniform opening, inspecting or donating to pagodas throughout the country. Another Buddha tooth relic pagoda in Mandalay had just been repaired. Interestingly, here the labour force was partly made up of *yebets*. These were convicts from the notorious *yebet sakahn*, or labour camps. It is believed that there were 110 such camps containing at their peak 50,000 to 100,000 prisoners. Terrible stories and photos of shackled labourers filled many Western journals. There were no photos of the *yebets* in leg irons in *The New Light*, just smiling soldiers being munificent by handing over a cheque for a juicy karma-dodging sum. Every photo was followed by a list of donors that read like a regimental roll call. It seemed that anyone who was anyone in the junta had to get onto the Pagoda Who's Who Donation List. The country should have been buoyed up by such beneficial karmic action, but this was not the case.

Mo and I drove on through the old British colonial area and past the famous Strand Hotel. All was in heartbreaking disrepair. The junta was not keen on renovating any reminders of colonialism; and, for reasons cited earlier, this sentiment was, to a degree, understandable. It was highly unlikely that any major general would want his name on the donation list for restoring the Pegu Club, that bastion of British privilege and symbol of foreign control. However, architecturally this was a tremendous loss to the city. We drove on to a development embodying the junta's idea of modernity: the Yangon City Central Plaza. Taking pride of place in the centre of the square was the concrete-and-glass Mingalar Cinema. It had recently been blessed by a visit from SLORC Secretary 1, Lieutenant General Khin Nyunt, the former head of military intelligence. Khin Nyunt, who was seen as the reasonable face of SLORC, was to go on to establish ceasefire agreements with seventeen insurgent ethnic groups. It seemed fitting that the cinema was showing *Robin Hood: Prince of Thieves* starring Kevin Costner. I'm not sure how Khin Nyunt would have dealt with the rebellious medieval axe handle, but I didn't think the choice of opening movie was auspicious for the junta.

Might it tap into the brooding dissatisfaction that ran through the nation? The SLORC was obviously sensitive to any stirrings of unrest and took every opportunity to urge the populace to toe the government line. Billboards bearing messages of almost 'Sinaic' gravity were everywhere. One impressive red-and-gold hoarding stated in Burmese and English, 'Love your mother and respect the law'. The twinning of these two sentiments escaped me.

The upcoming Thingyan Festival clearly worried the junta. Thingyan is the Buddhist New Year and traditionally involves the sprinkling of scented water from a silver bowl over friends, family and even strangers. This genteel practice is meant to wash away the sins of the previous year. Sadly, Buddhist Thingyan had now devolved into something much more bacchanalian and pagan involving the consumption of much alcohol, and dousing all and sundry with often dirty water spewed from hoses and even huge bamboo syringes. Pickup trucks full of drunken young men roamed the streets looking for victims, hurling gallons of water over anyone unfortunate enough to come within dousing distance. This was generally accompanied by much drunken singing and, from my subsequent experience, swearing, interestingly in English. Thingyan was a time to be avoided. It also contained the potential for social unrest and much axe-handling. With this in mind, the local Yangon SLORC had met to pre-empt any trouble. The meeting involved Brigadier General Thura Shwe Man, commander of the No. 11 Light Infantry Battalion; Colonel Tin Aye of Yangon Command; military region commanders; local regiment commanding officers; and the chairmen of the district and township SLORC organisations. The committee had enough manpower at its disposal to invade Thailand. They were obviously taking no chances. Warnings were posted: 'Punishment will be meted out to those who use unclean water, ice packs and water balloons injurious to others'. The brigadier general also warned against 'counter-culture modes of dress, drunkenness and attempts to exploit the festival for political gain, and… behaviour injurious to the State, persons and organisations'. It was pretty clear that, along with taming the drunken excesses of the bad boys on the pickup trucks, there was a clear threat to anyone who had political activity in mind.

Rangoon seemed to be a city in the midst of an identity crisis. Hoardings portrayed muscular citizens marching through fields of white flowers towards a unified, prosperous, and presumably axe-handle-free future. These images, which would have warmed the heart of the most unreconstructed Maoist, clashed with Western materialism. *Longyi*-clad figures, some smoking Burmese cheroots, waited in shady bus shelters covered with advertising for a 'racier' smoke: gaudy red-and-white posters for Lucky Strike – 'an American Original' – depicting a motorcycle rider roaring out from the hoarding on a Yamaha. An abrupt reminder of reality arrived when an ancient yellow bus, bursting with passengers, pulled up spewing black clouds from its exhaust, clouding the helmeted figure on the Yamaha, which disappeared like a lost dream. Sadly, the facades of impressive British colonial buildings sported much invasive greenery sprouting from windows and pediments. Flashy but insubstantial new high-rise apartment blocks were shooting up, their uncompromising hard lines and concrete jarring with the elegance of the neoclassical. A line of monks in simple maroon robes walked calmly in front of the huge face of Sylvester Stallone, replete with shades and automatic weapon. His blockbuster, *Cobra*, was doing the rounds.

Mo was eager to move on to something much more serious: urban clearances. This was all a bit sensitive, so if I left the car he would keep a distance. Through some sort of 'compulsory purchase', much of downtown Yangon was being rebuilt. Single-storey, colonial-verandaed houses were being torn down at the same time as the shiny new apartments were going up. Mo explained that many of the former inhabitants of the old buildings were being shipped out to the suburbs and the new apartments made available to those with the wherewithal to afford them. We passed the new Nawarat Hotel, owned by the daughter of Ne Win of 'number nine' fame, and then on to the new FMI shopping centre, where smartly turned-out Burmese were enjoying an air-conditioned retail experience. We wound up the day at the other end of the economic spectrum with a visit to one of the poorer areas just outside town. Virtually in the shadow of a new high-rise, a much more basic retail experience was offered to the poor in a warren of wooden structures. Everywhere was activity and clamour. A man in a red *longyi* and a baseball cap was selling water from a pail. Vendors with yellow-*thanakaed*[3] faces sat on the ground waving flies off heaped fruits and vegetables. Young men in stained singlets shouted to one another as they hauled heavy loads in baskets from a lorry. Families sat on low plastic stools under blue awnings, enjoying a meal. Elderly

---

3   *Thanaka* is a paste of ground bark applied to the skin.

pink-robed nuns with shaven heads browsed through the vegetables. This was several light years away from Stallone and Lucky Strike. And nearly everyone smiled as, very aware of my intrusion, I self-consciously took photos.

For Mo, Saturday was to be a serious highlight. It was time to see The Lady. Strict discipline had to be observed. He would take me to University Avenue where Aung San Suu Kyi remained under house arrest. As it was Saturday, she was allowed to address the crowd which would gather at the gates of her house. Mo thought it best for business if he kept his distance, and when we reached University Avenue he dropped me off at the end of the road. In front of me stretched what appeared to be the population of a Yangon suburb. They squatted on the road, some behind yellow crush barriers, most of the men wearing white shirts. It was early afternoon and the day was at its hottest, so a range of headgear littered the crowd: conical straw hats, towels, light scarves, baseball caps and, for those of a literary bent, books. Monks huddled in the shade of their dark burgundy robes; a jungle (if that is the collective noun) of axe handles! I turned to look back at Mo. He maintained his distance and signalled for me to go forward. Suddenly, two of the white-shirted men seized my arms, shoving and hauling me through the crowd to the foot of a blue metal gate about eight feet high. I was pushed down onto the pavement, and from somewhere a newspaper was thrown over my head. This was the People's Forum. At four in the afternoon Aung San Suu Kyi, the darling of the West, the hope of the nation, the People's Princess, would address the crowd. But how? The crowd was in good spirits, and tension mounted. So did the temperature. The gentle tinkling of bells from cool drink vendors floated through the heat. Sweltering under the newspaper, I tried to find comfort on the hot pavement. But this was a privilege: to be here with the Burmese people, at this moment in their history, and to have a grandstand seat. And then it happened.

A file of seven men in smart black *longyis* and white shirts, all bearing the red flash of the fighting peacock, the symbol of the National League for Democracy (NLD), appeared in front of the gate. On either side of them stood young men and women wearing salmon-coloured jackets: the Burmese *daik pon ein-gyi*. Suddenly, to a roar from the crowd, from behind the gate three figures emerged. They stood puppet-like, peering down at the crowd. Two men in the uniform white shirts and black *longyis* framed the slight, smiling figure of The Lady crisply turned out in a burnt orange Burmese top and a patterned *longyi*. Yellow orchids hung from her dark hair, creating a striking contrast. She was fifty years old but looked in her prime. Speaking with a smile and occasionally glancing at a script, she addressed the crowd through a microphone, which added a tense shrillness to her voice, heightening the already charged atmosphere. She smiled, the crowd smiled back; she paused in her speech, and they clapped and called back to her. She spoke with urgency and passion, throwing back her head, and they cheered and encouraged her. This was the People's Forum in action. With deep and intentional irony, the junta called it the Pavement *Hluttaw* (Parliament), and disparaged it through their media. To them Aung San Suu Kyi had been tainted by treacherously marrying a foreigner; to them she was an axe handle. To the people sitting on the pavement in the heat she was their *Daw Su*, the hope of the nation.

After speaking for an hour in Burmese she looked down from the gate and saw me holding a small tape recorder, and began to explain in English to me and any other 'foreign guests' what she had been saying. I was amazed as she explained, clearly and in cultivated tones, that, "The people are very concerned that there is no such thing as the rule of law in this country because the authorities have been acting in an increasingly lawless manner to the members and supporters of the National League for Democracy. We find that the people are concerned about such goings-on. Our people do not approve of injustice. Although they have been very much intimidated and repressed by the authorities, they still stand on the side of justice and peace. We are confident we will achieve our goal of genuine democracy. They also asked me to explain about fascism, possibly because the 27th March was the forty-third anniversary of the resistance to fascism during the war, and I had to explain what fascism means and how fascist governments operate and behave towards their people." She had used the example of the struggle for democracy which had taken place in the former Czechoslovakia.

I shouted my thanks to her and the crowd cheered and clapped, and the three figures vanished behind the gate as suddenly as they had appeared. Dusk was falling fast, and an orange glow settled, silhouetting the tall palms which lined the avenue. Young members of the NLD posed, laughing, for photos, and the crowd began to disperse with the cheerful atmosphere which is generated when people have shared an uplifting experience. It was almost a communion, a kind of sharing of a form of Eucharist.

The New Light had another opinion. The NLD was now ruled by 'politburo gang masters' and the mistress of the 'Pavement *Hluttaw*' was the '*Saya Ma-naing Hna saung-pyaing Ein-gyi-shin Ma Ma*' (the mistress of the two-winged great house) who, apparently, no black magicians can conquer. It was an impressive, Gothic description of the delicate figure with yellow orchids in her hair who had just spoken about democracy. I expect she would have charmed the magicians, black or otherwise, had they been there that day.

Three

Inspirations

Nats, Mabel and the Methodists, Shan State, Northern Burma, April 1996

The following day I flew north to Taunggyi near what was to become a favourite tourist destination: Inle Lake. The small plane landed on a grassy airstrip and I was met by a lady of middle years wearing a conical straw hat. She introduced herself as Mabel. "I'm Pa'O, the ones with the black trousers," she explained, establishing her ethnicity. This was clearly important. Defining the edges of identity is always important in Burma. In this case, black trousers were obviously vital. For the next two days Mabel showed me around temples, markets and a paper mill. However, it turned out that she was of a political bent too. She was delighted that I had seen Aung San Suu Kyi and complained bitterly about the conduct of the Burmese soldiers, who, she said 'bully the hell out of the locals'. Mabel's English was quaint, something of a relic of Empire; but Empire relics were everywhere in Burma, as I was to find on this trip.

Staying at the old British hill station of Maymyo (May Town, named after a Colonel James May) was rather bizarre. Mock-Tudor houses framed by well-arranged gardens stood in their own grounds on the hillside. At least one was under conversion into a hotel, and I was shown to a room by a young man wearing an oversized suit with rolled-up trousers. The moment I opened the door, the one thing that struck me immediately was the smell. All concerns and tensions seemed to fall away because this was the familiar smell of the England of my childhood, of my grandparents' front room, of wooden furniture. In place of curtains a piece of orange cloth was tacked over the window, gently filtering the light onto the scarred surface and carved legs of the solid wooden table. The huge sideboard still showed the burn marks from candles long extinguished. In Burma the past is always with you, not in the form of a cherished museum piece, but often something physically neglected yet somehow spiritually alive, asserting its presence on the affairs of the moment. Maybe places have a karmic force, too.

The British army had long left Maymyo, but it was now occupied by the Burmese army, which had moved into an extensive barracks on the edge of the town. Warming to her political theme, Mabel mentioned again that 'They bully the hell out of the locals!' I suspected that she was, in fact, a closet axe handle; at some risk she took me to meet an Italian priest who was very ill at ease with my visit and warned me against taking photographs in certain areas. Even here there were the usual Orwellian hoardings extolling the virtues of national unity and filial piety. This was Shan State and the British had 'ruled' here with a very light touch, as they had in the 'frontier areas' such as Chin and Kachin. The Shan's traditional rulers, the *Sawbwas*, continued to rule, with some overview from a local British commissioner. This arrangement seemed to work. "The Shan cry for the return of the British," Mabel explained with some passion, and went on to talk about the Panglong Agreement struck in 1947 between General Aung San and representatives of the Shan, Kachin and Chin peoples. The agreement guaranteed internal autonomy to the three areas. Aung San was assassinated in 1947, and the agreement was ignored by the military government when it finally took power in 1962.

Two particular incidents stand out from this visit. The first occurred in the town of Kalaw. Mabel took me to the market, a festival of colour where turbaned Shan dressed in gold, crimson, purple, emerald and deep reds, contrasting with the monochrome of Mabel's people, the Pa'O, in their black pyjamas and white turbans. A heap of baseball caps was, to me, a crass intrusion into the proceedings as the Shan in their elegant finery bargained, chatted and laughed. Two men, all in white, carried a large golden bowl suspended from a pole on their shoulders. Accompanied by a third, they collected donations for the local monastery. We followed them to a white staircase winding to the top of a rocky promontory where the monastery seemed to be precariously suspended. Nuns in pink robes sat on the cool stone steps taking whatever shade they could. A man in dark shirt and shorts squatted at a small table littered with a handful of objects. One caught my eye: a curious small metal figure with head thrown back, sitting on a lotus. Despite its size it was quite weighty, and red dust clung to its finely moulded contours. Mabel explained that this was the Law Ka Nat, the chief of the thirty-seven Burmese Nats, and thought the figurine was quite old as its fingertips were worn. Nat worship predates Buddhism in Burma and persists despite the general adoption of Theravada Buddhism starting in the third century BC. Some Nats, such as the Law Ka Nat, were brought into the Buddhist pantheon of Bodhisattvas. The Law Ka Nat became the Bodhisattva of Compassion, Avalokiteshvara, representing the continuous flow of Burmese spirituality stretching for over two thousand years. Overcome by non-Buddhist craving, I felt I really would like that figure, and asked the price. The seller pondered for a moment, took a deep breath and demanded some exorbitant sum. An uneasy silence prevailed. I sensed a brewing storm. Mabel was clearly having none of this. Suddenly transformed into a force of nature, she launched into an assault with dramatic hand gestures accompanied by shrill exclamations of shock and disgust. The man was soon browbeaten into agreeing to a reasonable price and hurriedly wrapped the Nat in newspaper and, with both hands, surrendered it to us. Quite traumatised, the poor chap retreated into the shade. The Law Ka Nat, the 'one who hears the cries of the world', has been with me for nearly a quarter of a century now, and sits on my desk as I write, defying my aspirations to develop Buddhist non-attachment.

That evening something most peculiar occurred at the small hotel where I was staying in Taunggyi. I hadn't seen a Westerner since leaving Yangon, and there had been few to be seen even there. I had been told that the Burmese were reluctant to speak openly to foreigners. Informers were everywhere. However, they desperately wanted to communicate with foreigners and say something about their lives. I was eating in the small hotel restaurant, which was furnished with metal tables and rather uncomfortable chairs, when I noticed that a lady, one of the staff, kept passing my table, lingering a little, then returning to the kitchen. Gradually the restaurant emptied of its few customers and darkness fell. In the low light, the lady approached me and said, rather uneasily and in good English, "I have something for you." She produced a small piece of lined writing paper and handed it to me. Pencilled on it in English, in perfect copperplate handwriting, was what looked like a verse. She glanced from side to side and then in a low voice began to recite:

Do all the good you can, by all the means you can,
in all the ways you can, in all the places you can, at
all the times you can, to all the people you can, as
long as ever you can.

Without explanation, like a passing memory, she disappeared into the growing darkness. She had just recited the prayer of John Wesley, the eighteenth-century English evangelist and founder of Methodism, the form of Christianity which had shaped my own childhood.

The next day, back in Yangon, Mo was as relaxed as, I suspect, he ever could be. He agreed to a beer before I left, and I thanked him for everything he had done and wondered if there was anything I could do for him. This seemed to trigger a bout of serious consideration. There was one thing he wanted. He hesitated. His reluctance was worrying; something awkward, perhaps even dangerous, was surfacing from the depths of his soul. Looking down at the table, he whispered, "Could I please have your photographer's jacket?"

Later, jacket-less, I reached the airport. I felt its loss; however, other less tangible but more substantial things had entered my life. I had the presence of the Nat, the spirit of John Wesley, and the inspiration of the slight figure with yellow orchids in her hair who, like the Law Ka Nat, threw back her head and heard the cries of the world.

Taking Stock

For Those Who Wish to Go Down This Path

You have to take risks. If you are not prepared to do so, then you will never walk this path. The first step is the hardest. Take it and the rest will follow.

Don't sing 'Kumbaya'! It's much too sentimental and sentiment can be misleading. See people as they are and develop compassion based on a sense of common humanity not on sentiment.

Four

Fight the Good Fight

British "Betrayal", Elephant Beer and Miners' Strikes, Mae Khong Kah Refugee Camp, Thai–Burmese Border/Seaham, County Durham, England, April 1998

"I called my son Winston, and you British, you betrayed us! What are you going to do?" The angry words were hurled at me by an elderly figure in a red, white and green Karen jacket. At that time the UK's Labour government was proudly presenting to the world its ethical foreign policy. I quickly abandoned any thoughts of attempting to explain this as the gentleman would obviously settle for nothing less than a regime change. However, having unleashed his passion on me as a representative of Perfidious Albion, and being totally, unashamedly and helplessly drunk, he sank to the floor and was soon asleep. This was understandable given the amount of alcohol he'd consumed over the night.

The gentleman was chair of the board for the Baptist schools in Mae Khong Kah camp, and had berated me about the dreadful deeds of my ancestors; the broken promises by British officers regarding British government support for Karen independence. "We helped you to fight the Japanese and you promised us our own country!" Over half a century later, the Karen still felt that betrayal deeply. It was now 1999 and three years had passed since my first encounter with them, but it still felt like 1947.

I had returned every year to Mae Khong Kah to deliver a short summer school for Saw Htoo Wah's pupils. The drinking party had been a big honour for me. Saw Htoo Wah's house was filled with about twenty men, all in red, white and green Karen dress, sitting cross-legged on the floor. The colours were highly symbolic, with the red standing for bravery, the white for purity and the green for loyalty. It was the green that had rankled with the elderly gentleman now snoozing on the floor. And the Karen certainly had a case. The civil war which had brought thousands of people to Thailand for safety had spluttered on for fifty years and the prospect of an independent state still lived in the imaginations, hopes and dreams of many Karen, yet seemed as far away as ever. Not that this had figured highly in the drinking bout. There had remained a little light in the sky as the drinks had arrived. I was quite taken aback because I had expected some kind of home-brewed rice wine. Nothing of the sort! From somewhere the Karen had procured a couple of dozen chunky British pint glasses with handles. These were presented to the assembled guests, followed by large bottles of green-labelled Chang (Elephant) beer. However, this was not exactly the drink of choice. It was, in fact, a mixer. Several bottles of Thai Mekhong 'whisky' appeared, and every glass was filled with half a pint of beer and topped up with half a pint of whisky! This was serious stuff, and clearly the road to oblivion. I was kitted out in Karen gear with *siplaw* (jacket) and *teku* (sarong), which Saw Htoo Wah's wife gingerly showed me how to tie in an adjustable knot at the waist. This was a huge honour, and I stumbled through some thank-you speech which seemed to please the guests, now well into their cups and with little grasp on reality. The night had gone well, apart from the spectacular finale from the chairman of the board.

Visiting every year for the past three years had given me an insight into the Karen and their plight. What struck me was the similarity between their village life and the life I had known as a boy in a County Durham mining village. Both were highly conservative societies prizing social cohesion. In the Karen villages, as in the mining villages, the local people policed their own communities. 'Problem families' were identified, the subject of much gossip, and generally avoided. Adultery was a cardinal sin. The Karen were particularly severe on this count, ostracising adulterers and eventually requiring them to make a public repentance. A few years later I was to see a young lady who had been found guilty of adultery forced to repent her misdeed in church to a congregation of perhaps two hundred people. It was uncomfortable to see her in tears on a stage, asking for the community's forgiveness. I'm not certain what happened to the man involved.

The church was at the heart of the community (in Durham it had been mainly the chapel), and in both communities places of worship were well attended, with everyone dressed for the occasion. The singing was inspiring. The Karen had adopted many 'standard' hymns and sang with great gusto and harmony, throwing themselves into the verses with heart and soul. 'Fight the Good Fight' was very popular, as could be imagined. I often thought that my grandmother, a fervent supporter of what could be termed the 'Hezbollah' wing of the Methodist Church, would have been quite at home in a Karen village. Interestingly, the Karen had been converted from Animism to Christianity mainly through the efforts of American Baptists, starting with Adoniram Judson in the 1830s. His task was made all the easier by the existence of a Karen myth about a light-skinned stranger who would arrive bearing a golden book. Added to this was their belief in a key spirit called Yaweh. This was not too far from Yahweh/Jehovah! Feeding into the Karen's long-standing hatred of the Burmans, the missionaries were even instrumental in arming them, and the Karen had been fighting their good fight ever since.

Both communities were also aspirational. Education was highly prized. Most families in Durham mining villages pushed their children to achieve, and grammar-school scholarships were much sought after and viewed as passports to a better education and a way out of the mines. Neglected by the central Burman state, the Karen too saw education as a way to build a better and possibly independent future. The British had offered this to cultivate their support. During one of my summer schools three boys had turned up. They could not get enough of the work and sat most of the night with me, practising their English. I was surprised to find that they were not from the camp but had walked three days from inside Karen State to attend. That said much about the state of things on the other side of the border. Tales came out of bush schools set up after the Burmese army had raided villages and burnt schools.

And strangely, both communities were now in the midst of some kind of identity crisis. At that time, I was working at the high school in Seaham on the Durham coast. A once quite affluent mining town with three collieries, it had been developed by the landowning Londonderry family into a port for the export of coal, and unlike other mining towns it sported some stylish neoclassical buildings from the 1840s. In Durham, mining died hard under the Thatcher government of the 1980s. An industry, which over two hundred years had grown, thrived, and spawned a whole way of life and language was, by 1995, dead. In fact, mining had been dying since the 1960s but the final coup de grâce delivered by the Tories in the 1980s had brought stiff resistance. The miners did not have an armed wing nor a warlord, but they did have the National Union of Mineworkers (NUM) and Arthur Scargill, which at times seemed to amount to much the same thing. Many refused to support Scargill's call to strike. The union members had not, in fact, been balloted, so many saw the Great Strike of 1984 as 'illegal' and unwanted. Tensions arose in communities such as Seaham between supporters of the strike and those who wanted to work. The latter were known as 'scabs', their names painted on walls and their route to work lined with angry, yelling strikers. Police were drafted in from London and there were some violent scenes. Karen communities were also split between support for the KNU and its hope of a Karen state and the Buddhist breakaway group the DKBA.

Retribution in both communities could be brutal, and in Karen State it was often lethal.

The villages of the old Durham coalfield were now in the process of reinventing themselves and new housing estates for commuters were planned for Seaham. 'Gentrification' and 'high-tech' looked to be the options for the future. Old identities die hard, and new ones can have a troubled infancy. The certainties of employment which the coal industry had provided were no longer there for young people. Seaham had contracted in all ways after the closure of the mines, and the effect drip-fed into the lives of its young people. The town maintained a residual sense of community but the seams, at times, looked to be coming apart. Male suicide rates were the highest in the country and young people were restive. Trouble flared up between gangs, and the police imposed a curfew. Cynicism poisoned the hopes of these Durham working-class communities which had been so aspirational during my own childhood. To me, as a teacher, this became a corrosive force; it seemed to eat into the very fabric of the school itself. A squat concrete structure, built in the 1970s to last no longer than twenty-five years, it was now nearly thirty years old, and the concrete was crumbling. Chunks of it fell out of the classroom walls, and door and window frames were loose. The physical decay of the school seemed to mirror the social decay of the wider community, and sometimes it felt as if the whole building would gradually sink into some old mineshaft. Fortunately, the head teacher, Bob Dingle, was energetic and go-ahead and rather liked the idea of twinning the school with its Karen equivalent, or near enough. This was done, funds were raised, and letters were sent. Generosity was still intact despite the circumstances. Saw Htoo Wah received enough money from Seaham School and other sources to buy a TV set, a satellite dish and a solar-powered battery charger. The Karen at Mae Khong Kah now had a window into the world, and, hopefully, my own pupils could become involved in something much bigger than themselves.

There are times when one sits back and enjoys a few moments tasting the seductive fruits of achievement. This is dangerous. Nemesis, the inescapable agent of your downfall, is watching for just such an opportunity. The link with the camps created one of my worst experiences as a teacher and could have led to a national 'incident' which would probably have cost me my job, and career and had a serious knock-on into the wider educational world. Even now the prospect of explaining what happened many years ago leads to a rise in my now increasingly volatile blood pressure.

My class of 14 year olds, in the then pre-computer age, had set up a pen-pal link with their counterparts in one of the refugee camps. This was good stuff, it was a worthwhile activity which fed into a sense that schools should be engaging with the wider world. We got that engagement in spades but perhaps not as the well-meaning educational planners had intended. It was not long after 9/11 and the popular press was running a series of sales-boosting scare stories. Al Qaeda was likely to launch an attack at any time. Britons should be alert. Osama Bin Laden look-alikes were appearing everywhere. But, it wasn't all unfounded as there had been anthrax attacks in the USA.

On a sunny morning in late 2001 a parcel of aerogrammes from Thailand had arrived and there was much excitement in the classroom at this first exchange which promised a venture into unknown lives. At the end of the lesson, with theatrical gravity, I distributed the crumpled blue envelopes. The bell rang and the class was dismissed. They made for the door... and then a girl turned and poured out a small pile of white powder from the folded aerogramme. There are moments etched into one's memory, vivid, stubbornly defying attempts at erasure and of such enormity that mind-numbing paralysis becomes the preferred option. In fact, that was my default state for the rest of the day, and the week, as the members of the fire-brigade in 'space-suits' were called to check the powder. I knew all along what it was, I told myself, it was chalk-dust. We were covered in it at the end of every lesson in the camps. The Karen were issued with soft chalk, about the consistency of dry cheese, to scratch text onto rough bamboo boards, and the dust was everywhere. But this was England in the throes of an Al Qaeda scare stoked up by the tabloids. The 'space-suits' found that the dust was, in fact, chalk. Interestingly the real threat and scare stories continued for some years with *The Sun* newspaper in 2010 suggesting a possible attack on the set of the nation's favourite soap opera, Coronation Street.[4] In 2019 a woman found a shell on the beach at Winchelsea which apparently looked like Osama bin Laden!

I never mentioned the incident to the Karen. They would have been mortified. Over the years the relationship between the British and Karen pupils grew and fears blew away; dare I say, like dust in the wind.

---

4   'Al Qaeda Corrie Threat' *The Sun*, December 9th 2010 .

Five

In and Out

Dangers, Jane Austen and a Night March, Thai–Burmese Border, 1997–1999

"In the morning my heart is like a melon. At night it is like a pea." One Karen described his growing fear over the course of a day in these terms. And fear was ever present in the camps. Attacks were a constant threat.

My forays into the Karen Hills from '97 to '99 became personal 'multipurpose expeditions'. From being a small boy I had had a passion for history, and that was, in fact, my motivation for taking on photojournalistic projects for Rex. I loved the adventure of it all, but also I could bring much back to my own community. I was at heart a teacher, and when possible I brought my experiences of the wider world back into the confines of the classroom. The truth of the matter was that I was a much better teacher than I was a photographer, and the Karen situation offered me a chance to be both. I could turn my experience of teaching to much good use in the camps, and create a photographic record of history in the making. I could also bring these experiences back to my pupils, who were, in fact, living through their own period of what would come to be seen as historic change.

I did not actively seek volunteers at this time, partly because of the risk of attacks on the camps. At that point I did not want that responsibility. Volunteers would come in time. Doing occasional photojournalistic work for Rex had given me some experience of working in war-torn areas. As a young man I had lived and worked in Papua New Guinea and was prone to taking off into the bush and living with the locals for extended periods. I had been with the Philippine Rangers and 20th Air Commando in northern Luzon during an offensive against communist guerrillas, and I'd seen a fair share of human distress in Nicaragua and Cambodia. Although I was a seasoned traveller, sometimes the growing sense of fear in the camps and my personal isolation brought me to the edge of panic.

On one occasion there was much concern in Mae Khong Kah that an attack could be imminent. Attacks usually came at night with small groups of armed men rushing into the camp and setting fire to the thatched houses. The impact of this in such a confined area would be devastating. That reality came home to me one evening. Walking with Saw Htoo Wah through the darkness back to my house, we were suddenly confronted by a file of armed men moving silently through the night, almost invisible in their black shirts and shorts. There was a tense moment as the leader stared at me in surprise. Saw Htoo Wah quickly explained that this was the perimeter guard, and they were on the alert. They paused briefly, rather taken aback, and then hurried on at a trot into the darkness. I climbed the ladder into my house and, feeling that I ought to be prepared for the worst, packed all my essentials into a camera bag and my rucksack and waited. Floating through the darkness came a Karen hymn, the voices strong and strangely calming. Suddenly a section of a house burst into flames. Screams and shouts replaced the singing. At points like this you may not feel inclined to theorise on the existence of a deity who may or may not agree to work in your interests if you petition Him (or Her). Let me assure you that blind faith is the sensible option. My unashamed response was to recite what I could remember of the twenty-third Psalm. Quite quickly the burning structure collapsed, the flames died down and a tense stillness lingered, broken only by the crackling of smoking timbers. I had lost count of the times I had walked 'through the Valley of the Shadow of Death' and sat listening, staring into the darkness. The night passed without further event.

Actually, getting into Mae Khong Kah had proved to be something of an operation. The Karen did not favour the dried-up riverbed approach but preferred something more direct, which meant taking a vehicle through a Thai checkpoint. The Thais, in general, put up with Karen comings and goings because they saw them as useful, if disposable, allies. The Karen National Liberation Army (KNLA) used the camps for R & R and continued a desultory fight against the Burmese. The camps were, in fact, a buffer for the Thais against a rather predatory Burmese military government. Reputedly known as 'the girls' by the Burmese army, the Thai soldiers, according to some reports, didn't come out too well in any clashes. They did not want to die for the

Karen and therefore saw 'the moles' as a better option for the front line in any firefight. This was the Burmese army nickname for the Karen soldiers who seemed to disappear into the ground. Added to this was the very useful network of Karen informants who kept both Karen and Thai forces up to date with information about Burmese troop movements. In spite of all of this, the Thais would not allow stray foreigners into the camps. Even NGO workers could only enter to deliver goods.

The Thais therefore had to be avoided, and the Karen had just the system for doing so. Heading along the dirt road into the hills towards Mae Khong Kah, the pickup truck in which I was riding stopped in what seemed to be the middle of nowhere about one hundred yards short of a bend. I was told that a Thai army checkpoint was just ahead, and having a *gollowa* (Karen for 'Westerner') in the truck would cause problems. I left my gear on the back of the truck and, together with Saw Htoo Wah and two others, began a circuitous walk through the hills towards the 'tradesman's entrance' to the camp. The hills of the Dawna Range were dry, and the track, covered in crisp brown leaves, ran along the edge of a ridge through groves of spindly eucalyptus. At this height the air was fresh, and the clear skies allowed quite spectacular views across the folds of tree-covered ridges into Burma. Occasionally we came across whole areas that had been burnt and cleared with a few charred trunks standing like rotten teeth. Slash-and-burn was common practice in the hills, and one could see the beginnings of organisation prior to cultivation as the logs of felled trees were stacked in neat racks. Saw Htoo Wah was not impressed. He surveyed one cleared area and muttered, "Bad family." The general organisation of the felled trees was not to his liking. Drawing on my vast experience of slash-and-burn, I nodded sagely. One of the men with us was Kaw Wah, a strong, sinewy Karen who, it turned out, was something of a football star. His house was full of trophies which he had hauled with him to the camp. The thought of hauling a sack of football trophies over a mountain range beggared belief, but some things are literally priceless. Pointing out a stream running through the gully at the bottom of the slope, Kaw Wah came out with that delightful Karen word for stream, *ti klo*. The word captured the music of the running water and was echoed in the magic of the vistas opening up on either side.

After a lunch of boiled rice and vegetables we moved on through the hills, encountering one group of Karen from the camp squatting in a clearing. This was obviously a stopping-off point for the back entrance to the camp, as discarded plastic bottles and cans were dumped under the trees. This is a sad facet of something which in later years I noted had become endemic in Burma. Travellers had an almost complete disregard for the environment, hurling plastic bags and bottles out of the windows of vehicles, and whole areas around villages were covered in this debris from the modern world. However, at that time, the camps were almost free from the curse of litter. Plastic bags were considered valuable reusable objects, and many could be seen drying on the bamboo roofs of houses.

It was a four-hour walk into the camp and Saw Htoo Wah's wife had copious amounts of lime juice ready for us on our arrival. On that visit I was housed in a kind of dormitory kept for single young men. I was given a couple of blankets and noted that, thankfully, this room had a chair. Pinned to the bamboo wall was a huge poster of a naked Asian girl. The young men of the dormitory had obviously felt that I would appreciate the company on what are bitterly cold nights in the hills. In these circumstances, taking a bath also becomes something of an art in the maintenance of personal modesty. The Karen bathe every day at twilight by sluicing themselves down in public with cans of water taken from a large drum which stands outside most houses. Dignity is maintained by keeping yourself wrapped in your *teku* while pouring water over your head and body. On this occasion my efforts to wash with the required level of dignity became something of a spectator sport, drawing the attention of the local children, who hid behind a bush to watch the *gollowa*'s clumsy efforts to keep his *teku* in place. It was all the more theatrical as I had to do this balanced on a bamboo platform at the back of the house. Some rather stern Anglo-Saxon comments flushed the voyeurs out from the nearby rustling bush.

Getting out of the camp was much more hazardous than getting in, but at least I could get out. This is one of the problems with getting involved in situations such as this: you take risks, they take risks, but you leave, and they stay and suffer any consequences if they have crossed a line as people taking refuge in a foreign country. In fact, the Karen were not by international legal definitions 'refugees'. Ten years previously I had been in the huge camps set up by the Thais on the Cambodian border to take in the influx of refugees following the fall to the Khmer Rouge and the Vietnamese invasion of Cambodia. These were vast bamboo towns run by a special border force designated to 'control the

Khmer'. Some of the camps were also run, in reality, by the deposed Khmer Rouge and other armed political factions. Did the Thais at that time see the camps as providing something of a buffer against expanding Vietnamese influence in the region and its initially hard line communist model? It was certainly a widely held opinion that the Karen were being used as a buffer against a burgeoning Burmese military regime. Whatever the macropolitics, it is easy to see Thailand as something of a beleaguered country in an unstable region. This was compounded by the fact that Thailand itself was intrinsically unstable, with short terms of relative democracy superseded by military coups. In 1997 it had achieved a level of stability under the government of the former head of the Royal Thai Army, General Chavalit Yongchaiyudh. It ran a policy of political expediency, protecting its borders while portraying itself as a protector of the displaced. And displacement was evident throughout the region. I was never certain how the Karen calculated the mood of the Thai border force that had posts up and down the border but not in the camps themselves. They controlled the main roads and some of the back roads. The mood and severity with which rules were applied could change quite quickly, very often depending on how the central government wanted to portray itself in its dealings with the refugee situation. Fairly easy-going attitudes could be quickly replaced by stringent measures, or at least threats of stringent measures.

On one occasion I was delivering a summer school for small groups of Karen pupils. At that time the Thais had decided on a census. All the Karen were to report to a certain point in their camp for a headcount. They did this with great dignity, lining up in their national dress. It would have made a wonderful photographic opportunity except that I was confined to a room at the back of a house and told not to leave. My main concern was that I had succumbed to an old smoking habit and the smell of tobacco might alert any Thai soldiers checking the houses for census evaders. However, as a kind of benign 'minder' the Karen had sent a young man called Sha Htoo to join me for the duration of the headcount. He smiled cautiously, and his eyes seemed to reflect in turn sadness and curiosity. Covering the back of his left hand was an elaborate tattoo in blue ink which looked almost Celtic in its intertwining complexity. Within the hour, some light was shed on this. The two of us bundled up in the back of the house and waited quite comfortably in the shade. The Karen love to sing and Sha Htoo was no exception, and he had a guitar. Karen is a lullaby of a language, coming in breathy tones from somewhere deep inside. In a low, light voice, he sang about a child who had woken in the night and was coaxed back to bed by his elder brother; a comforting domestic scene, but Sha Htoo's life had not been so comfortable, and some nights had been very threatening. A desultory conversation began to develop in which, haltingly at first as he retrieved English words long unused, he told his story. The DKBA and SLORC troops had arrived in his village and forced men, women and children to be porters for them. This included Sha Htoo's father. His cousin had been shot to death – "when he was in a hut," Sha Htoo said with a faint smile. This is typical of the Karen: they smile and often laugh at their own misfortune. It seems almost callous to us at times but it's how they handle pain. The villagers eventually fled across the Salween into Thailand, thinking they were safely settled in Pi Thi La camp. Their safety was shattered when the DKBA attacked the camp. "They came in the dark, one o'clock after midnight." Sha Htoo struggled to find the words. "They caught our leader Saw Weh Klo and brought him back to Burma. They needed him because he was the head of the refugee leaders." Sha Htoo's father was now too old to work and his mother was the main breadwinner and had become something of an entrepreneur, buying vegetables in a local Thai market and selling them in the camp at a profit. She made about 50 baht (90 pence) a week. However, her son also had a particularly interesting skill which had earned him something of a reputation. I had been told that Sha Htoo was a designer, but what could he design in a refugee camp; what had marked him out as such a specialist? What was the product by which he had cut his reputation at such an early age? The answer was hand-painted pillowcases. Sha Htoo had with him a large, bound black book of his designs, and showed it proudly. Inside was page after page of designs based, as far as I could tell, on nineteenth-century English samplers of almost Jane Austen vintage. Gothic script garlanded in flowers of yellow, ochre and light green declared, 'Forget Me Not', 'Never Leave Me', 'You are My Beautiful World', 'Home Sweet Home' and, for those whose attachments were of a less worldly nature, 'Jesus is My Saviour' and, with a shower of hearts, 'God is Love'. These were creations of intricate and somewhat baroque beauty, all skilfully drawn freehand. Despite the brutality of his world Sha Htoo had produced items of delicacy, their simple human sentiments bringing comfort in day-to-day adversity. By now I was no longer shocked by cultural incongruity or the almost heartbreaking paradoxes. This was the Karen world. They bore their suffering with smiles and lived in the twilight of an Empire which had forgotten them, but whose presence still lingered in the shadows, a continuum of a reality that was almost tangible. Sha Htoo and I sat quietly in the fading light of the late afternoon, waiting for the Thai soldiers to leave. I smoked my last Marlboro Light and he struggled with a copy of *Two Years Before the Mast*. Sha Htoo could arguably have written a better story.

The Thais were definitely having one of their tightening-up times. They never lasted, but you had to look sharp for a while. If getting into the camp during one of these crackdowns had required a long hike through the hills, then what would getting out entail? I was soon to find out. It was 2.30 in the morning and, in the cold and the dark, a group of about a dozen young men gathered at Saw Htoo Wah's house. It was a clear night and we mustered by the light of a big moon. An oil lamp inside the house brought some comfort as mugs of hot tea were handed out. There was a clear sense of excitement and tension. The plan was to walk out of the camp, follow a stream past the Thai army post and join up with a truck somewhere at the other end. Complete silence was to be maintained and torches were not to be used.

And so we lined up. Kli Shi, a sturdy young man, slung my backpack on his shoulder, and in single file we began our walk downhill through the camp. By moonlight it was just possible to see the outline of the man in front of you and follow the swaying of his shoulder bag. The main sound was the flop of sandals against bare skin but from the hills came the whiplash sounds of the tree lizard and the occasional *choc-choc* of what the Karen describe as a 'wide-mouth bird': the nightjar. We made our way through the houses, their thatched gables silhouetted against the moonlight, and then the pace slowed: we had arrived at the stream. Despite the rains it was fairly shallow, and the cold water lapped against our calves as we made our way out of the village and into the stands of bamboo. Here was the point of tension: the Thai army post stood to our left against the light of the moon, and the line slowed as, carefully and as silently as possible, we made our way past the low-lying buildings along the stream, feeling for stones underfoot; a fall would have been disastrous, the loss of a sandal a hindrance to the whole line. The swish of feet through the water, the swinging bag of the man in front, the feel of sharp stones against rubber sandals, and then we were past and gradually the pace quickened and we scrambled out of the stream and onto the opposite bank. Two pickup trucks waited, and we piled aboard. A sense of relief was followed by the inevitable Karen laughter as we drove off into the night.

Six

Forgotten Friends

Old Soldiers, Lost Lives and New Hopes, Mae Khong Kah Refugee Camp, Thai–Burmese border, March–April 1998

A bright-eyed old man sat cross-legged on the floor below a poster of a bearded figure in Karen dress, looking at a black-and-white photograph of a young man in military uniform. The photograph lay beside what appeared to be some kind of certificate bearing a name, a military rank and a large black spider. Half a century of Karen history was in that scene. The bearded figure in the poster was Saw Ba U Gyi, the Cambridge-trained lawyer and founder of the post-war Karen independence movement. The uniformed young man in the photograph was the old man fifty years ago. Pa Aye Hay was ninety-six years old. He remembered his army number, 45643, and had served under Major Campbell. The spider was the symbol of Force 136, a network of Karen guerrillas who'd fought against the Japanese under

British officers. The unit was cunningly disguised as Force 361 in the book *The Bridge Over the River Kwai* and its film adaptation *The Bridge on the River Kwai*. In the latter the Karen were airbrushed out of history, replaced by 'our loyal Thai allies'. The Thais had, in fact, supported the Japanese. Our real allies had been the Karen, and many of those soldiers were now conveniently forgotten and living out their last days in refugee camps, hoping for their pensions.

Colonel Edgar Peacock had been in charge of the operations in which Pa Aye Hay had been involved. Peacock was certainly a man of the Empire (born in India, spending his early life in the Forestry Commission within Burma), and when the war broke out he was commissioned into the Special Operations Executive (SOE) responsible for espionage, sabotage and reconnaissance. In 1944 he led Operation Character in Karen State and was tasked with raising and training units of Karen. Pa Aye Hay was a *naik* (corporal) in one of those units and described himself as 'a simple soldier who has to follow according to command'. He was involved with reconnaissance and sabotage, and described to me one of his missions to locate a Japanese airstrip. Its whereabouts were conveyed back to the British, who then bombed the strip. He spoke with great respect about his immediate commanding officer Major Campbell, describing him as 'a good man who loved the Karen very much'. Working in the ethnic regions I have come across this theme of a bond with the British time and time again, one unfashionable in contemporary Britain but spoken about openly in the ethnic regions, often followed by comments about a deep mistrust of the Burman government which succeeded the British and against whom many of the ethnic groups are still waging a war. One sometimes has to stand back from one's liberal prejudices and see the world through the eyes of those whose experience is very different from one's own. One tends to see the world through a prism fashioned in the intellectual heat of one's times and the past becomes the victim of judgement based on current values and the seemingly moral certainty of a contemporary perspective. This can be, at times, misguided. British involvement in the world over the past two hundred years is in many circles seen as malign. Talking to the Karen and other ethnic groups in Burma, one encounters a very different perspective. 'Truth' is often elusive and history is invariably complex. One needs to be cautious of selective interpretations of history made to suit a contemporary political agenda. When the British left after the defeat of the Japanese, Pa Aye Hay expected that there would now be peace. Nothing could have been further from the truth. For him the worst was yet to come in the form of the communist insurgency. "These were the worst times, even worse than now," he told me, as the communists eventually turned on one another and on the Karen.

The one issue that concerned Pa Aye Hay now was his pension. He had heard that the British government had sent money to the Burmese government to be given to those who had served in the British army. The problem was that he lived in an insurgent area and was reluctant to go to Yangon and make his claim for fear of being arrested. I said I would do my best to find out about Karen pensions when I returned to England. I later contacted the War Office with details but heard nothing back from them. I often wondered how Pa Aye Hay viewed me after having known Campbell and Peacock, but found it best not to go down that road. To an extent my generation lived in the shadow of Empire and its heroes. But eventually we did other things and remained loyal to the Karen for the next twenty-five years, sharing Campbell's sentiments.

I have always found the stories of old soldiers fascinating, including those of my own father which I more or less knew by heart by the time I was ten years old. My father's war had ended in 1945 and that memory was becoming history. He had lived to enjoy the benefits of his struggle and I had been fortunate enough to grow up in a welfare state with secondary education, free healthcare and substantial housing for all. Pa Aye Hay's war had never really ended, and he was seeing out his days in a refugee camp. War blighted the future of the young men and women wanting to rebuild their nation. For them frustration and desperation were setting in, as I was about to find out.

It was a cold morning and, in the grey of the dawn, I wandered out of my bamboo house. I was preparing to leave and stood on the hard-beaten earth of the court the young people used for playing *takraw*, a kind of kick-volleyball. People were stirring, coughing in the sharp morning air, and fires began to glow from house to house, filling the air with the smell of woodsmoke. Suddenly, out of the half-light a figure moved quickly but carefully towards me. He was clutching something in his arms. I recognised the lightly bearded face of Saw Ywa Hay. The previous night he and I had sat with a tape recorder as he related his story. Saw Ywa Hay was twenty-eight years old and a refugee with a wife and three children. He had moved to the KNU-controlled area in 1991 to escape SLORC control, and had become a mathematics teacher in Hti Moo Kee village. Sitting cross-legged on the bamboo floor, holding a sheet of paper, he'd bent over the recorder and with great care read his moving story. With a clear sense of audience, he'd opened with the statement, "My name is Saw Ywa Hay and I love democracy. In the first week of December 1997, SLORC soldiers attacked my village, burnt houses, rice stores and all the school materials. Two villagers and three KNU soldiers were killed. When I heard the SLORC were coming I ran away before the attack. My home is very far from the Thai–Burmese borderline to walk. I start my travel village by village, and passed the jungle and Salween River to the refugee camp. When I am travelling, I had two sons, my wife is seven months pregnant. It was difficult for my wife to walk. My daughter was born here. I carried some blankets and two pots for cooking. When I arrived here the camp gave me two blankets, three pullovers, rice, fish paste, and yellow bean month by month to eat. I cut the bamboo and built the house by myself... My job is teaching. I teach maths. On February 21st, 1997, when I heard the news by BBC Norway RFA[5] about the SLORC caught my father U Saw Htoo and use him as a porter to carry their rice and bullets. The SLORC killed him in the jungle. My father is seventy-five years old and the second chairman of NLD Taungoo Township, Burma. He tried with Aung San Suu Kyi for Burma democracy. I also pray may God bless you forever."

His story had filled my thoughts during the night, and now he stood in front of me as the light began to reveal the

---

5   Radio Free Asia.

white bundle in his arms. The bundle began to stir as he offered it to me. "This is my daughter. Please take her with you."

I was numb with frustration. What Saw Ywa Hay was feeling was incalculable.

Seven

A Bird Has Two Wings

**Reality Bites, Green Screens and Soft Porn,
Mae Khong Kah Refugee Camp, Thai-Burmese
border, April 1999**

After four years of visiting the camps and delivering short summer schools I had grown to respect the Karen. They were hospitable, kind and brave, and I liked them immensely. They were also human beings, with all that means. I was never sure what they thought of me.

I found that I was in something of a cultural conundrum. Western culture prized individuality and creative and critical thinking. It had a dynamic often emanating from the young and aspirational. All of this was reflected in its education system. Older people could be seen as a conservative drawback. Karen, and broader Burmese culture, worked in a different way. Essentially it was much more conservative, with cultural transmission being very important, especially through history. Teachers, and older people in general, were highly respected and not to be questioned. Corporal punishment in schools, a no-go area in the West, was accepted.

Gradually, I had begun to see what I could usefully bring to their schools. Karen pupils learnt everything by rote. Facts and figures were instilled by repetition and choral chanting. It was almost impossible to hold a conversation near a school due to the noise. But it was ordered and focused noise, and very unlike the chaos you could find in some classes in England. Teachers were well respected and rote learning had its place but, as a teacher myself, I knew that a good teacher needed a repertoire of skills to meet a range of purposes and audiences. I had survived various waves of educational ideology in England, from 'child-centred discovery' favoured by those of a liberal bent to 'man at the front', which a local Conservative MP told me he really wanted to see. They followed the zeitgeist of the time, which might be liberal, authoritarian or, from time to time, borderline transcendental. What seemed like a good idea from someone in a think tank became a headache for a head teacher and often a nightmare for the overworked teacher at the 'chalkface'. Teachers were not ideologues but, in general, pragmatists. They had to hold the interest of classes, which could range from the studious to the semi-feral, cover the content of a syllabus, meet exam targets and maintain a reasonable level of personal sanity. They did this by adopting and adapting accordingly whatever bright idea came from above.

At this point, I made the dreadful mistake that actually served the work we were to do in the future very well. I hit on the idea of buying in an English language course complete with videos which could be played using the equipment bought by my school at home for the Karen. The BBC had one such course, so I invested some money in this and brought it out to Mae Khong Kah with some pride. I gave some demo lessons to teachers so that they could see how the course could be used, but teachers used to using techniques of rote learning and recall find it difficult to adopt and adapt more 'communicative and active' styles. It became depressingly obvious that in order for the exercise to be successful it would take intensive teacher training over quite a period of time. At the time it felt like I had wasted time and money, but I was to see this again and again over the coming years with many well-intentioned but flawed projects, and when, ten years later as a fully fledged educational charity, we were asked to set up an English language course in the camps, we did it carefully with continuous training, regular classroom support, and the development of customised course materials. This left a trained workforce in place with materials it could use. It took us five years to deliver that project, and that was time well spent.

Working with the Karen pupils, I had tried to introduce active ways of using the language, such as pair work, group work, a little drama and filmed news broadcasts. They loved filming *News from the Camp*. It wasn't heady stuff, with missing pigs and other stories focusing mainly on livestock making the headlines. One year I tried a photographic project. I had attempted to get moody photos of refugees looking glum or in some way inhibited, which I thought gave some idea of their situation. I distributed small cardboard Kodak cameras to a team of pupils and asked them to go off and document their lives. Secretly, I hoped for some telling shots in the social realist style which would come up well in black and white. The Karen were not of the same frame of mind. The pictures showed:

- Lots of family and friends looking self-consciously at the camera.
- Individuals with pets and ducks. Ducks were a big favourite.
- Young men with guitars posing as rock stars.
- Young women standing in front of Burmese glamour posters.
- Cats.

The values seemed, in a way, universal, and for a social scientist I was sure that these photos would be very revealing at some point in the future. The football shirts would be of special significance. As a Western photographer the temptation is to objectify other humans and see them as something 'other', exotic, unusual, exploited, dispossessed. I had undergone a personal change. I had come to know the Karen as 'real people'. They were individuals with names and histories and friends and families, and now when I raised my camera to take a picture it was not of 'Typical Karen woman preparing rice', it was 'Naw Klo Htoo making dinner for the family'.

The TV equipment had gone down well. The whole system was linked to a generator which rattled and whirred from six in the evening until ten. With Reithian zeal I had hoped that it would bring the world into the camp, educating, informing and perhaps a little entertaining, but it wasn't me who selected the viewing. I discovered that a new phrase had been coined: 'The screen is green'. I puzzled at the meaning of this until it was explained to me that when the Karen wanted to watch the news on the Burmese channel (run by the government), all they could see were soldiers parading around, building pagodas and inspecting factories! Lighter viewing was required, and topping the popularity polls was *The Simpsons*. However, more adult tastes were catered for.

I stumbled across some 'alternative' viewing when one night I found Saw Htoo Wah's house packed with men sitting in silent anticipation. The Karen had managed to tune into a French station showing a programme featuring some risqué visual humour involving a diminutive Hercule Poirot figure and a cancan dancer. I had no idea if money had changed hands, but I began to see how this could, at some point, be the case. Another lesson: what might seem to be your philanthropic bright idea becomes someone else's business opportunity. As the charity grew, we were to meet this local 'entrepreneurship' time and again. It is very easy from a Western point of view to condemn those who take advantage of services that are meant to be given freely, but this must be tempered with a certain level of understanding. The Karen, like all ethnic groups, have their 'big men' who are seen as providers not just for their immediate family, but often for a network of extended family and friends. This role, which comes with much status and responsibility, is in general accepted as part and parcel of local social structure, but although a small NGO must understand local custom and practice, a judgement must be made as to when tradition moves into the realm of exploitation. For me this first brush with potential low-level exploitation was a sobering and, I have to say, quite depressing experience. What had been a bright and shining quest had become tainted by the reality of survival. It forced me to readjust any rather precious ideas I might have had about the nature of my relationship with the Karen, and put it onto a more realistic footing. Looking back, it all seems rather amusing and what is actually quite ridiculous is my own naivete, but it felt so different at the time. I sat smoking and brooding in my small hotel room in Mae Sariang, feeling as if I had been somewhat duped. It was all self-indulgence; people living in precarious situations will do everything they can to survive. The Buddhist assertion that a bird needs two wings to fly and these are called wisdom and compassion is a pretty good guide in these circumstances. With wisdom you see the world as it really is, and temper that reality with compassion. I pulled out of my reality blues and moved on.

My suspicions of 'opportunism', however, were soon borne out by further developments. In the year 2000 we were invited by a Karen official to deliver a summer school in the much bigger camp of Mae Ra Ma Luang. An old friend from my days in Australia and New Guinea, Bill Arnerich, a teacher from California, offered his services, as did two teachers I had met at a showing of the film *Welcome to Sarajevo*. Steve Newman worked in a tough school in Sunderland and Paul Stephenson (not his real name) taught in Newcastle. Both were involved in local Amnesty International groups. The threat to the camps seemed to have diminished but I was still a little apprehensive about taking a team out with me to Mae Ra Ma Luang. Nevertheless, suitable preparations were made, a course put together, and we were ready to go. We were to find our own way to Mae Sariang, where we would be picked up by the Karen. It would be a five-hour trip by four-wheel drive to reach the camp deep in the Dawna Range. All seemed possible until the intervention of the 'entrepreneurial spirit'. Shortly before leaving England, I received word from the Karen official that the trip would cost us $1,600. This was exactly the amount my school and a branch of the local Labour Party had raised to support education in Mae Khong Kah. I was flabbergasted! We had expected to pay for the transport, but this was, to our way of thinking, pure opportunism. I wrote back with a sharp refusal and began to make alternative arrangements. The official changed his mind and dropped the request for this exorbitant sum. Subsequently, he and I became good friends, but this first attempt to take a team out to the Thai border was nearly the last, with consequences, as I will explain, that were almost fatal.

Taking Stock

For Those Who Wish to Go Down This Path

See people as they are. You will be dealing with people living in precarious situations. Don't get disheartened if they seem self-serving and you feel you have been exploited. We are all human and will do what we can to survive.

Show and feel compassion for others, and don't forget yourself. As already mentioned, don't base your compassion on sentimentality but on a sense of shared humanity – be wise and see the world as it is.

The work you do is very serious, but don't take yourself too seriously. That road leads only to delusion and to danger.

Remember, in the end you can always leave. They can't. Don't sing 'Kumbaya'.

Eight

A Near-Terminal Experience

Bribery, Manchester United and French Friends, Mae Ra Ma Luang Refugee Camp, Thai-Burmese Border, April 2000

'The ground came up to hit me' is an expression often used by writers to create the dramatic sensation of sudden physical collapse, and it is entirely correct. I can confirm that the experience is violent, shocking and totally disorientating.

In my case, the ground rose after I lowered myself from the back of a pickup truck following a five-hour ride to Mae Ra Ma Luang camp in the Dawna Range. The rest was confusion. My face hit the hard red earth; I felt hands lifting me under my arms and my legs dragging along the ground and then banging against the rungs of a ladder. I was hauled onto a bamboo-slat floor and then a leaf mat. I fell in and out of consciousness. Faces, Karen and Western, loomed over me, blurring in the white haze. Sometime later I was to find out that the cause of my collapse was a blood clot which had developed in my leg and moved to my groin, from where a piece had broken off and hit my lung.

Coming into consciousness, I heard someone whispering over and over again in my ear, and felt a hand stroking my arm. I was not sure what was being whispered but became aware of a young Karen man kneeling beside me. The rhythmic stroking continued, and then the words, which one would have expected to be some kind of protective mantra, gradually became clear. "Manchester United, Manchester United." Even in my semi-conscious state the evocation of the spirit of Charlton, Best, Law et al. brought a surreal sense of comfort. A Karen lady clambered into the hut and squatted down beside me. I felt the tightness of a blood-pressure band on my right arm and heard her working the pump. I am rather at a loss to explain the deep motivation behind the action that now occurred, as it bordered on the ironically absurd. For a number of years, I had taught a unit in my media studies course at my school in England called 'Images of the Third World'. As part of this, pupils looked at how the 'developing world' was represented in film and photography. One image that was repeated time and again was that of the white doctor and the native patient. Local people were rarely shown as having any agency in these affairs, and I needed an image which reversed the situation. I now had one, but I had not intended for myself to be the patient. Flat on my back, being tended to by a 'native medic', I was excellent course material for GCSE media studies. It was a photo op too good to miss, and even in my semi-comatose state I realised this. I called to Bill to take the photo, but he refused, saying he didn't like photographing me in this state. I insisted and

Bill reluctantly took the shot. Twenty years later I keep it in my office along with a small bottle containing the blood clot; a gruesome reminder of mortality and a reason to give thanks.

At the time I didn't know what the actual problem was and only later found out about the blood clot that had lodged in my right groin. The whole of my right leg quickly swelled and stiffened. I recovered enough to start the four-day course with around seventy Karen teachers, but the only relief I could find was lying on the floor with my leg on top of my camera bag. After a day my leg was taking on an elephantine shape and the pain was excruciating. How had all of this happened? In Thomas Hardy's novels the development of the plot sometimes hinges on a small, accidental incident or a haphazard brief encounter. The cause of my rapidly swelling leg was one such. A few weeks before I had left England my doctor had noticed a distortion of my right calf and mentioned that in years to come I might have some circulation problems. The problems had arrived more quickly than expected.

One week earlier, sitting in a cafe in Mae Sariang, we had been joined by a Karen of middle years sporting a long moustache. This was Baw Poh, Mae Ra Ma Luang's camp leader. He explained to us that we would be leaving early in the morning and that all had been 'arranged' with the Thai camp commander and guards. 'Arranged' actually meant 'bribed'. What we were doing was entirely 'under the radar' and required a certain oiling of the wheels. But in this case oil was not the lubricant of choice; honey was. The commander's wife apparently had a sweet tooth, and so the Karen had searched the woods for something appropriate and come up with a bucketful of wild honey. All would now be well. However, our problems were to come from the functioning of a different mechanism.

The following morning the Karen sent a four-wheel drive to bring us from Mae Sariang. It was a smart vehicle, much better than expected, and the four of us had comfortable seats inside the cabin with our gear stashed in the back. All was set for a relatively comfortable journey. Spirits were high and there was much of the usual blokeish banter and ragging. One of my main concerns had been the safekeeping of a small photocopier which I had entrusted to Paul. After about an hour of driving into the hills the driver indicated that something was wrong with the brakes. On examination this turned out to be a small defective brake valve. It was not thought safe to continue and would take a couple of days to repair in those circumstances. Being on a rather tight schedule, we didn't have a couple of days to spare, but the solution arrived a few hours later in the shape of a battered blue pickup truck containing several Karen along with their bags of rice and vegetables piled in the back. Faced with the prospect of five hours, at least, in the back of a cramped pickup, we accepted our fate, threw our gear into the truck and climbed aboard. The Karen made room for us, but four Westerners with equipment (including the precious photocopier) need a lot of room. We were packed tight and my legs were, more or less, jammed up to my chest. Even more Karen were taken on board further along the road. The photocopier disappeared somewhere in the scrum under sacks of bananas. The journey seemed endless and there was no relief for my legs however I tried to manoeuvre them.

After five hours we began a steep and dusty descent into Mae Ra Ma Luang. The dirt road is almost sheer, and without good brakes the consequences could have been dire. Some of the Karen jumped out as we neared the camp and there was a little breathing space. Paul, thankfully, still had the photocopier. Bill, who had been rather concerned about how his family would feel if they realised where he actually was at this point, was now in great spirits. There was no check by the camp guard. Presumably, they liked the honey. As the truck lurched into the camp in clouds of red dust, Bill stood up and I joined him behind the driver's cab. My head began to feel light and my legs weak. The truck shuddered and stopped. Our host, Lah Say, and a group of men in red sarongs (on reflection, obviously Manchester United supporters) ran out to meet us. And then the ground came up to hit me.

The last thing the Karen wanted was a dead *gollowa* on their hands, and several days later, when the seriousness of my condition was realised, the only thing to do was to get me out as quickly as possible. Luckily, a team of medics from the French organisation Aide Médicale Internationale (AMI) were due to visit the camp. Their mottos were '*Aller là où les autres ne vont pas*' ('To go where others don't go') and '*Aidons-les à se passer de nous*' ('Help them to do without us'). There were certainly no 'others' besides Bill, Steve, Paul and me in this neck of the woods, so they would be surprised to pick up a Brit with a gammy leg. I certainly couldn't do without them, and, what's more, they were Karen. More stereotype-breaking photo ops loomed large.

Steve joined me in the AMI truck, and we clattered out of the camp with the Beatles' 'All My Loving' playing on the truck's sound system. Several hours later, in the dark, we pulled into Mae Sariang Hospital's car park. The hospital was full of people who in the main looked to be local tribespeople: turbaned and tattooed, probably Thai Karen. A teenage Thai girl carrying a pink-and-blue backpack in the shape of a bear came and sat beside me. "I am a doctor," she announced quite sternly. It felt like a death threat. She was learning her trade in the medical badlands and I could be an 'interesting' patient. However, thankfully, the AMI medic (a Karen man of middle years) and a senior Thai nurse looked at my leg and now varicosed groin and, shaking their heads, decided that the solution was a swift evacuation to Chiang Mai. I was all for that.

I remain grateful for the advice of one young man. He was one of those quite remarkable characters you meet from time to time on the edges of what we often call 'civilisation'. These are almost characters from a Joseph Conrad novel who have taken up residence with the hill tribes of Southeast Asia. One such was Scott O'Brien, a young Canadian whom I had met three years previously while sitting in a Karen house in Mae Khong Kah camp. Scott had become more and more involved with the Karen cause and helped establish the Karen Teacher Working Group (KTWG). At great risk, these Karen teachers carried out teacher-training sessions inside war-torn Karen State. Scott had told me that, in an attack on a training centre, two teachers had been hanged. Training teachers was obviously a capital offence. Scott turned up to see me at Mae Sariang Hospital and advised me to go to Chiang Mai Ram Hospital or I could be butchered elsewhere. It was good advice. Within three days I was on an operating table in Chiang Mai Ram, where a sizeable blood clot was extracted from my groin. Two weeks later I was medevacked back to the UK, reunited with my long-suffering wife Jan, and given two months to recuperate, a course of injections administered by the district nurse and warfarin and surgical stockings to bring down the swelling.

The damage was serious and permanent. I would be left with a distended right leg for the rest of my life and it would require regular hospital visits for circulation checks, daily doses of blood thinners and the wearing of rather inelegant surgical stockings. Above all, knocks to the leg had to be avoided. This put an end to jogging and, sadly, to my weekly five-a-side football matches. Worst of all I was told never to fly again. The implications of this were devastating. There had always been tension between the project and home responsibilities. My periods out of the country had not been easy for my wife and I look back on those times with much, often uncomfortable, self-scrutiny. The pronouncement by the surgeon now seemed to have put an end not only to the project, but to any air travel. However, I took further advice and a possible solution emerged in the form of blood-thinning medication carried in a syringe and frequent in-flight exercise. This was not as bizarre as it might seem now. Thrombosis on long-haul flights had become a media issue and in the future I was to see passengers administering anti-coagulants with their own syringes. Thankfully, this would not be my fate.

More sobering news followed. I was now back in my 'alternative reality' of head of English at Seaham School of Technology, and the head teacher informed me that the school had just been notified that a team of Ofsted inspectors would shortly be arriving to carry out an inspection. A shadow hung over the school. Stress levels amongst staff were at an all-time high. Ofsted inspections were notoriously rigorous and could break careers. The past weeks of refugee camps, dusty roads and hospitals disappeared in a flurry of preparations for what would be four intensive days of classroom observation and grilling over results and course development for me and my team. Nevertheless, I knew all would be fine. Standing in my office looking at the grim clot of congealed blood in its plastic bottle filled me with gratitude for my extended grip on mortality and put Ofsted into perspective. Furthermore, I had my new life-saving mantra to call on. With the memory of the gentle whisper of 'Manchester United', we could face anything.

Aung San Suu Kyi and security April 96

Pah Aye Hay Force 136 Veteran

KNLA Unit Moei River 2004

Junta Signboard

'True Till Death'

Mae Khong Kah Camp

Salt delivery Mae Khong Kah Camp

KNLA Patrol

Karen School News Team Mae Khong Kah Camp

Mine Victims Mae La Camp

Author suffering from blood clot Mae Ra Ma Luang Camp

Monks Tham Hinn

Graham McNeil (centre) and Steve Newman (left) help to haul vehicle out of Mae Ra Ma Luang Camp

Katharine May Mae La Camp

English lesson Mae La Camp

Migrants making 'Illegal' crossing of Thai Burma border

Moving On

2000–2008

In 2000 while working in Karen refugee camps we set up a charity called the Karen Education Partnership (KEP). In 2006, as our programme began to expand to other ethnic groups, we changed our name to the Burma Education Partnership (BEP). Partly to allow for greater flexibility, it was later to become Mobile Education Partnerships (MEP).

Altruism is infectious, especially if it is laced with the flavour of adventure. For eight years starting in June 2000 we sent volunteer teams into the camps along the Thai–Burmese border. Recruitment was never a problem, and in those years we took round about seventy volunteers into the camps to deliver summer schools. They were all self-funding and the majority were practising classroom teachers. Right from the start we determined that lessons would only be delivered by qualified teachers, while others who wished to join us could work as classroom assistants. Teachers from all over the north-east of England (and eventually other parts of the country) volunteered, and organising the teams became a major undertaking. On a Friday night we finished in our schools back at home and on Saturday we were on a plane to Thailand.

Very quickly we found that summer schools were in demand in camps right along the border, from Htam Hinn, a tightly packed community baking in the open plains of the south, through to the northern camps of Mae La Oon and Mae Ra Ma Luang in the freshness of the Dawna Range. Everything had to be timed perfectly so a team could arrive in its designated camp at a given time to deliver the course, usually over four to five days, and then be out to rendezvous with the other teams in Chiang Mai or Bangkok and, after a day's R & R, get the plane home ready to start work again on the Monday. The whole operation took just under two weeks. The pressure leading up to these trips could be quite fierce.

These were formative years for us, and we learnt lessons. We were outsiders from the liberal West entering a very conservative community. High standards of behaviour and etiquette were vital. Lurid tales of the behaviour of drunken Westerners living in the camps filtered through to us, so we set a strict code of conduct and a dress code for all volunteers. Above all, we were determined right from the start to set high professional standards. As the organisation grew over the next few years, this attitude stood us in good stead. For a small organisation, credibility is everything.

But things are never quite what they appear to be; a theme to which we will return later. People may be altruistic but first and foremost they are human beings and, as such, will have their own agenda and work in their own interests. Valued friends can become difficult competitors. Unknown to us, two former trustees and one existing member of the board set up a similar organisation using contacts they had made through us over the previous years. We were suddenly faced with a charity based in the same area in the UK, with a similar name, working in education in the refugee and migrant communities on the Thai border, and potentially competing for similar human and financial resources. This came as a shock. For a small organisation trying to become established it was a blow from which it would take us time to recover. I include this not as a condemnation, but as a warning to all those who would follow the path of building an organisation. Beware of human ambition (including, of course, your own).

However, something much more positive began to take shape, and that was the formation of a core team, some of whom would stay with the charity for years. The variety of the team was essential to the organisation's future development. Graham McNeil, a shrewd and able Scot, brought the valuable capacity to think outside the box. Miriam Addy, sometimes the only female in a border expedition team, was meticulous in planning and adventurous in spirit. Graham Mortimer, who had lived almost nine years with the Karen, offered enormous knowledge and prudent advice. Sue Hawley added leadership skills and took charge of a team. Chris Crick brought skilled management and good judgement enriched by a deep sense of humanity. Steve Newman's astuteness laced with sharp wit kept our feet on the ground. Abby Boultbee lent the brightness and enthusiasm of youth, while Jo Burton brought the wisdom and compassion which grows out of lived-experience. A final (for the moment) and key addition joined us in the shape of Clive Taylor, a former deputy director in the British Council and projects manager for the Asia-Pacific area. He offered extensive knowledge, profound experience, and a gift for cutting through obstacles with sharp creativity. If still short on finances, we now had our team, and the shared endeavour cemented a camaraderie, a friendship, that survived the rigours to come. For many, these trips had been life-changing experiences. My life had already changed, and it was about to do so again.

Taking Stock

For Those Who Wish to Go Down This Path

Reflect on the capacity of ordinary people to do extraordinary things. Make your work challenging. People are boundlessly altruistic, but they also have a sense of adventure, and so do you. Recognise this and enjoy the motivation it brings.

You'll need a variety of relevant skills in your team, but make sure it includes people who will take initiative and responsibility. You can't do all the work yourself, but always go the extra yard for your team.

Watch out for human ambition. Once people know the ropes, they will want to go their own way. Don't be surprised if you wake up one morning and discover that there is another organisation that looks like a rip-off of your own. That's life.

Don't sing 'Kumbaya'.

Nine

Add Your Light to the Sum of Light

Jail, DUCK and the Dump Skiers, Mae Sot, Thai–Burmese Border, August 2008

Mo Mo had been arrested six times but, in between spells of incarceration, she rather enjoyed her life as a teacher in Mae Sot. She was an illegal migrant escaping the poverty and oppression that prevailed in military-run Burma. Thousands had crossed the border to find work in the paddy fields, the sweat shops and even the municipal dumps just inside Thailand. The migrants brought their kids and the kids needed education, so, following the law of supply and demand, ramshackle schools had sprung up all over the town of Mae Sot, which, with its corrugated-iron-and-plank buildings, espoused a retro-ramshackle look itself. This was punctuated by bizarre attempts at neoclassical buildings with concrete Corinthian columns often painted in garish reds, yellows and greens and sporting signs in Chinese.

Mae Sot was a border town and, in spite of its rather neglected appearance, was full of pickup trucks doing cross-border 'business'. It was also a magnet for mercenaries, missionaries, migrants and some interesting misfits. Migrant schools were set up anywhere. Disused shop-houses; old, abandoned properties; the top floor of a house – all could be quickly converted into a space for some form of learning. In spite of the harsh reality the names of the schools were aspirational (New Light, New Day, Sky Blue), or based around rather impenetrable acronyms such as BHSOH (Boarding High School for Orphans and Helpless Youths). Mo Mo's school had thankfully evaded the curse of the acronym and had adopted the refreshing name of Pyo Kin (Growing Plant). It also seemed to have unconsciously embraced green issues, as it was an ingenious assemblage of recycled materials: planks, bamboo, corrugated iron (a luxury) with gaps plugged with plastic sheets, cardboard boxes and anything else at hand. Children sat on straw mats on the floor behind long benches used as desks. Mo Mo lived in a corrugated-iron lean-to attached precariously to the school. The whole construction looked to be on the verge of collapse. Immediately outside, a green swamp gave a semi-rural feel, and could have added something to the whole Pyo Kin ecosystem had it not been covered in discarded plastic bags. In the rainy season it burst its banks and oozed into the classroom. In the surrounding area, the migrant families lived in worse conditions.

The school was actually one room containing about a hundred pupils with no partitions between the classes. A group of about a dozen youngsters who made up the Grade 4 class occupied one rather hot and dark corner.

Their teacher was conspicuously absent, and some of the pupils toyed with their textbooks while others sat idle. The teacher was in jail. Like ninety-eight per cent of Burmese teachers in Mae Sot, she had no ID papers and lived under the constant threat of being picked up by the Thai police and incarcerated until a fine was paid. The fine stood at about 500 baht; quite a hefty sum for staff paid maybe 2,000 baht a month. The town jail was one barred room open to the street and usually contained up to twenty people at any one time. Walking past, one felt something of a voyeur as the inmates sat in huddles, staring at a flickering TV set attached to the wall. The programmes were usually Thai game shows which, one assumed, were part of the punishment. Relatives visited and pushed plastic bags, often full of brightly coloured drinks, through the bars. The Grade 4 teacher was eventually released and returned to Growing Plant seemingly undamaged by game-show exposure.

This school was lucky in that it had one qualified teacher: Mo Mo. At that time there were, in fact, only thirty-nine qualified teachers in a workforce of four hundred and fifty-seven catering for eight thousand pupils in the Mae Sot area. Another twenty thousand migrant children of school age didn't even go to school, but worked in the paddy fields and sweatshops. I was informed that there were two hundred legal factories in the area, and two hundred illegal ones employing children between the ages of ten and fourteen. Child trafficking was also rife, with many children finishing up in the sex trade in Bangkok. Teachers often travelled with their children on the bus journeys home to provide some protection. However, word had it that some parents paid traffickers to take their children to work in Bangkok as 'flower sellers'. The going rate was 11,000 baht (about £200), which included bribes at checkpoints. The 'flower selling' had to be profitable to account for the outlay.

Mo Mo was in her early thirties, spoke some English, and had at one time kept ten cats. Five had died and a sixth, a mangy black tom, was clearly on its way out. Although the school, catering mainly for Muslims, was officially headed by Thein Htun, a bearded imam figure, Mo Mo ran the show. She was bright and cheerful, had an infectious giggle and was always well turned out in the classic Burmese style with cream *thanaka* circles on her cheeks. Her cats and the kids received most of her affection. I met many people like her over the years, and it was always a humbling experience. A number of years later I found out that she was living in Oklahoma.

What was my reason for being in Mae Sot? The answer lay in the fact that for the first time in the charity's history, we had some funding, which had allowed us to establish a longer-term programme. The wonderful students of the Durham University Charities Kommittee (DUCK) had agreed to give us a grant of £5,000 to work in the migrant schools of Mae Sot. DUCK is an amazing organisation that – by involving hundreds of students in sometimes bizarre, occasionally alarming, but always hugely successful fundraising events – raises thousands of pounds for charities every year and sends out 'expeditions' to different parts of the world to work for a few weeks with needy communities. In this case they intended to send an expedition to Mae Sot's migrant schools to help build playgrounds. Our charity, now the Burma Education Partnership, was part of the broader support. This first small grant was a start; it was, for us, a king's ransom. We could now put a team into the migrant schools for a period of three months. It was also the beginning of a long and fruitful relationship with the students of Durham University.

As a pilot exercise we had recruited three young teachers, Tina Bowler, Janina Wilson and Ollie Franks, to provide support in the migrant schools. This was not as easy as it sounds. For one thing, the schools were not recognised as schools by the Thai authorities and were instead designated as 'learning centres'. This gave them a kind of semi-permanent status as the migrants themselves were semi-permanent. The Thais were caught in something of a quandary. One reason for this was that they benefited from the migrant labour and many Burmese children actually attended Thai schools, but Burmese parents wanted their children to have a Burmese education so that they could fit into the Burmese system on their return. The result was a kind of uneasy stand-off, with the learning centres having to comply with Thai rules. These involved singing the national anthem, displaying a picture of the king, flying the flag and teaching some Thai language. Western volunteers were also banned, so we would have to take care and keep a low profile. Representatives from Thai immigration made spot checks to make sure the Burmese were complying. This seemed to cause tension with the local Thai education authority, which saw the value of the migrant schools as they took some of the burden of educating from them. Nevertheless, spot checks were carried out by uniformed officers and were much feared as a bad report could lead to closure. One school's rendition of the national anthem fell short of the required standards and, to add to their woes, it was also discovered that they had a Canadian volunteer. The young lady was quickly sent home. Under the threat of another spot check, choral singing now took priority within the curriculum. For the next few weeks, when passing the school at any time of the day, one could hear, floating through the hot air, the sound of Burmese voices butchering the Thai national anthem.

A second problem was that the teachers had little or no training and usually fell back on traditional methods. These generally involved rote learning drummed into young heads with choral chanting. This was excellent for recall but less so for understanding. It was not uncommon to ask a pupil, "What's your name?" and get the reply, "What's your name?" Active use of English was not really part of the system and questioning the teacher was off limits. Teachers had huge status in Burmese society and the Burmese word *saya* (teacher) is used to indicate anyone with learning or authority. Western techniques such as group discussion, textual analysis, pair work etc. were just not on the radar. Textbooks issued by the Burmese government also required this kind of traditional teaching and learning style, and this was enforced by exams based principally on recall. Head teachers, wary of their status being undermined, could be highly conservative, and a crusty head could intimidate a 'progressive' young teacher. So much care had to be taken. We were involved with a culture and a mindset, not just a system.

Perhaps new materials could provide a richer educational experience. Again, this was not as easy as it may seem, as I discovered when paying a visit to a school on the outskirts of the town. 'I go skiing' was the response chanted by the Grade 4 class in response to the teacher's prompt from a flashcard showing a figure with a flowing scarf descending snowy slopes. This was followed by 'I play baseball' and 'I go skateboarding', leading into a list of other chorused activities fairly familiar to a Western audience. Outside, the scene was almost post-apocalyptic. Heaps of rubbish formed a small range of hills around the school. Plastic bottles, cans, old shoes, wrappers, bags, boxes and the indefinable leftovers of modern life created a surreal, fly-infested landscape and a bizarre setting for the lesson. Looking rather like clumsy skiers, figures with scarves masking their faces and pointed sticks in their hands ranged over the rubbish. Skiing was out of the question. Scavenging, however, was definitely in vogue. This was 'the Dump', home to the children of Sky Blue school and their families. The name has an aspirational, almost other-worldly feel about it; the reality was less inspiring. The Dump's inhabitants were Burmese migrants who made a living out of selling whatever they could scavenge from the local tip. They were illegal, and I was told that their shelters were periodically pulled down by the Thai police. Life was precarious for the 'Dump skiers', so the teachers at the local school were using basically the same rote learning techniques from a batch of newly donated textbooks featuring Westernised lifestyles. Growing Plant and Sky Blue schools encapsulated the experience of the small migrant schools springing up around Mae Sot. They were at once bizarre, tragic and inspiring.

'What then shall we do?' These words haunted me over the years. I had originally come across them in C. J.

Koch's fine book, *The Year of Living Dangerously*. They are from Chapter 5 of the Gospel of John, and are quoted in Koch's book by Billy Kwan, a cameraman who is moved by the poverty he witnesses in Jakarta in 1965. His solution is seminal: you must 'Add your light to the sum of light'. You can't change a situation on your own, but you can add whatever you can to the good works that others do. The problem is discovering what your light really is and using it well, or at least as well as you can. This would be central to the quest which was about to consume us all.

Ten

Looking for Something to Believe In

Gods, Mercenaries and Lost Souls, Mae Sot, Thai–Burmese border, late 2008

Ship me somewheres east of Suez, where the best is like
the worst,
Where there aren't no Ten Commandments an' a man
can raise a thirst.
(*Mandalay* by Rudyard Kipling)

'Find It, Fuck It, Forget It!' were the words emblazoned on a camouflage-green T-shirt worn by a young man with cropped hair. His pal, with a long ponytail, did not share his romantic sentiments but, similarly, sported a camouflage shirt and tan combat trousers. I assumed they were mercenaries, or possibly photographers wanting to link up with the Karen just across the border. They sat sipping coffee at a table outside a small cafe called, with a suggestion of snug intimacy, Coffee Corner. However, the setting contradicted this assumption. Western vulgarity clashed with Eastern spirituality. From the walls of the cafe the Hindu gods stared down sympathetically on customers. A purple figure of Shiva, the destroyer, with trident; a pink Ganesh, the elephant god, carrying a lotus and an axe; and a blue-and-yellow Vishnu standing on a pink lotus added spiritual grace to the mundane mechanics of dining. Buddhist chants glided out of a speaker and the transcendental aroma of incense mixed with the everyday smell of frying eggs.

The other-worldly atmosphere was suddenly broken by a more prosaic 'G'day, mate'. Dan had arrived for a chat. Dan was an Australian who, although still relatively young, had a face full of stories and they hadn't all been happy ones. He always gave the appearance of being on the edge of something – something new, something dangerous or just something else. Dan chain-smoked, and when not actually drawing on a cigarette, had one placed seductively on the table. He seemed to be testing his will. His trembling hands were continually drawn towards the prize, and despite efforts to the contrary he always gave way to the temptation, hurriedly lighting up and inhaling deeply. I liked him. I liked his Aussie expansiveness and his generosity of spirit. Above all, Dan was a great raconteur. He had been a journalist and was now a professional Karen enthusiast, engrossed in writing a book about their struggle. He had found his cause: the Karen Revolution, their struggle for independence and self-determination, the preservation of their culture so threatened by the Burmese military. His loyalty was affirmed by a large red, white and blue shield framed by bull's horns tattooed on his right shoulder. This was the symbol for the KNU.

Dan's enthusiasm for the Karen cause clashed somewhat with the world view held by his Thai wife, Phu, the proprietor of Coffee Corner, who was a devout Buddhist with a penchant for some of the Hindu gods. She had had an interesting spiritual journey, having once tried Christianity but subsequently given up the Ten Commandments for the Eight Precepts and this colourful mixture of Buddhism and Hinduism. I never figured out how it worked but her deities all seemed to get along well, with Phu favouring specific gods for specific purposes. Ganesh was a particular favourite.

While Phu cultivated her other-worldly relationships, Dan had more mundane contacts in the KNLA. He wanted to make the cafe their Mae Sot HQ. With that in mind, he'd decided to fortify Coffee Corner. The room adjacent to the coffee shop was a hive of activity, with workmen busy installing large sheets of black bulletproof glass. This would make a splendid in-town office for the new Karen leader, Ner Dar Myar. Assassinations were not unknown in Mae Sot. A few months earlier the KNU's secretary general, Padoh Mahn Sha, had been gunned down on the veranda of his house by two men apparently bearing baskets of fruit as gifts. According to Dan, Ner Dar Myar had a 10 million baht bounty on his head. That's a lot of fruit.

The Karen had been having a hard time over the past few years and, according to Dan, now controlled only a strip of land adjacent to the Thai border. In Burma spiritual leaders emerge from time to time, amass a following, and lead them headlong to their inevitable doom in some kind of holy war. The Karen had had such an experience with the Htoo twins, Johnny and Luther. The boys, aged about ten, had gained a following after defending their village against an attack by the Burmese army. Eventually, legend had it that supernatural powers were attributed to them, which apparently rendered them immune to bullets and landmines, and able to manufacture magical bullets. They initially attracted a following of about five hundred fighters calling themselves 'God's Army', and were allegedly involved in some quite audacious exploits including the seizure of a hospital in Ratchaburi, Thailand. This was pretty desperate stuff, and doomed to failure once the 'magic bullet' game was rumbled by their rapidly decreasing numbers. In 2006, with their group having shrunk to about twenty armed men (who were presumably grateful to be alive), the twins surrendered. Luther finished up in Sweden, where he studied economics and liberal studies and worked in a care home for the elderly. I wondered if the residents knew about his life-preserving powers. A route to immortality would have been tempting and he could have raised a loyal, if ageing, following. Johnny ground away some years in a refugee camp on the Thai border. It's a tragic and crazy story but gives some idea of the desperation faced by the Karen. But messianic leaders come with a health warning anywhere in the world.

Despite their setbacks Dan was as devoted to the Karen as Phu was to her gods. The cafe, standing opposite the best hotel in town, had become a conduit for all and sundry. Every morning at Coffee Corner was an adventure as a cross section of everyone attracted to the Karen cause filtered through the cafe, enjoying scrambled eggs and coffee and a chat with Dan. Customers included aid workers, mercenaries, missionaries, lost souls looking for a cause and those on the political fringe. The following morning the fortifications were almost complete. Sacks of camouflage gear were stored behind the bulletproof windows. Sleeping bags and mosquito nets awaited seven or eight soldiers to join up with the KNLA's 5th Brigade in Papun. Dan was well pleased. I loved his stories, even if some did stretch reality in a rather colourful manner. But this was Mae Sot, where reality could take on an alternative dimension.

One morning, a small group of Westerners was sitting at one of Coffee Corner's outdoor tables beside a pink statue of Phra Mae Khong Kah, the goddess of water. I introduce the divinity as her serene gentility contrasted with the hostile appearance of a group at a nearby table. They were Italian, and a number wore blue T-shirts emblazoned with a stylised white horse and rider. One T-shirt bore the cryptic name Zetazeroalfa and another Popoli. Tattoos were in vogue. Something Gothic was inked into the back of a young lady's neck, and others sported broken-bottle leg tattoos and a range of rather odd geometric symbols. It all looked very pagan. And they were lightly armed. The group had gathered around a heavily built man with a shaven head, and were admiring his rather ugly knife as he fingered its serrated edge. "Medics," whispered Dan. Medics?! Was the serrated-edged dagger in fact a surgical instrument? Was Zetazeroalfa an antimalarial drug? It was some years later that I found out that Popoli was a group which was part of an international network linked to the Italian neo-fascist organisation CasaPound and Zetazeroalfa was a neo-fascist rock group. According to the International Institute for Counter-Terrorism (ICT):

The common thread that connects these organizations is their clear international vocation and activism, frequently disguised as humanitarian aid and solidarity toward 'those people fighting for their survival'.

The network was or had been involved in South Africa, Burma, Kosovo, Palestine and Lebanon, and from 2013 would support the Assad regime in Syria. 'Those people fighting for their survival' in this case were the Karen, and the role of 'medics' delivering supplies fitted the story. I never figured out what Phu thought about all of this: insurgents in the annex, neo-fascists on the terrace and mercenaries in the parlour. Buddhist non-attachment was advisable. However, Phu had another vocation. She was the local oracle.

This all came out a couple of days later. The Coffee Corner club had a new member: a tall, rangy Belgian with a long ponytail and a winning, innocent smile. This was Raymond[6], a war photographer, and he suffered from severe speech and hearing impairment. Dressed in full camouflage combat gear, he sat around most of the day, smoking cigarettes and holding desultory conversations by notebook with whomever was around. He was waiting to hook up with the Karen. Photographing war means photographing human distress, and this presents us with a problem. As fellow human beings we need to be able to justify our actions or face a loss of self-regard and a coarsening of spirit. Raymond's presence prompted my own memories.

---

6   Not real name

I once witnessed a man die of wounds. It was the first time I had undertaken photographic work in a war-torn area, and it led to much self-examination. It all happened in the bare yard of a hospital in Jinotega on the Nicaraguan–Honduran border in 1983 during the Contra War. A truck pulled up and a group of soldiers gently lifted down the body of a wounded man onto the cracked concrete yard. He'd been hit by shrapnel, and cotton wads were stuffed into the wounds on his bare legs, but the bleeding could not be stopped. A nurse held him in her arms and tried to raise his head, which rolled back against her shoulder and then fell limp. She stared at me, her gaze filled with a human and moral question which I feared to answer. Gripped by the enormity of the emotional conflict involved in photographing the scene, I hesitated, turned to walk away and then quickly released the shutter. He was a fine-looking man, and I felt ashamed. Black dogs sniffed around the yard in the fading evening light. Such is the banality of death. For a while the memory of taking that picture haunted me like a secret crime, but it stood as part of a true record of the times. To ignore the event would have been the poorer option.

What attracts a person to areas of conflict? Over the years history had drawn me to these dark places, and whenever I travelled I met men and women from all walks of life, beckoned by some calling, mixed perhaps with a sense of adventure, to record, to document and to give something of themselves in these margins where some of the great human dramas are played out. Maybe, to paraphrase what I believe the great war reporter Martha Gellhorn said, we don't need someone to lead us out of the desert; we can't get enough of the desert. I admired Raymond's determination, especially given that he lacked two physical senses. I hope the pictures he took never robbed him of his sense of common humanity.

Image was important to Raymond, and from somewhere he had procured a high-powered camouflaged motorbike. This had proved irresistible to the locals, who are usually confined to Honda 125s or equivalents. With delight and amusement, the proprietors of local small shops, perhaps sensing revenge, watched as the overweight rent collector hauled himself and his moneybag onto Raymond's bike and began tearing around the square outside the cafe like a war god.

Phu and I were rather enjoying the plight of the rent collector, who seemed bent on serious self-harm, when a well-dressed man approached and asked if Phu was 'open'. Strangely, although the cafe was obviously open, Phu replied, with a smile, "*Yang*" – not yet. On enquiring why she was 'closed', she told me that the man wanted his fortune read and she preferred to do this later in the day at a more auspicious time. This was Phu's second calling: predicting futures and helping people to, among other things, make good business decisions. Now I understood the reason behind her array of Premier Division gods. I was rather taken aback when she offered to look into my own destiny. Books and charts were produced, and dates of birth and other details checked against complex astrological tables. After some deliberation Phu declared, with Delphic authority, "Your god is Shiva." I rather liked that idea. Shiva, the Nataraja, the Lord of the Dance who brings change and destroys ignorance. He sounded like a good bet. This was followed by, "Your duty is to help people." Now, my vanity was vast enough to ignore any latent scepticism and swallow up Phu's pronouncement. So, rather cheered – or deluded – by divine approval for my philanthropic mission, I awaited the final pronouncement on my destiny. Another check of the astrological tables led to a profound pause, and then, with a sharp rush of breath, "But no one can help you." I knew there would be a catch – there always is with oracles; just ask the Greeks. This sounded ominous, as did the climactic statement, "Only God can help you," delivered with the grim finality of a life sentence. Vainglory rapidly giving way to desperation, I decided that this called for some serious petitioning. I was not totally certain to which god Phu was referring from her extensive pantheon; could it be the Lord of the Dance? Events, as we shall find out, were soon to take a hand in this.

Our team was doing well. Tina, Janina and Ollie had settled into their schools and we were working out how to solve some of the day-to-day problems. Our quest was to find the best way to use a small team of trainers in the most effective way given the scale of the problem. The model we had come up with was proving to be quite robust: with our team of three we would form a mobile unit of teacher trainers. Each trainer would be allocated a small cluster of schools and would work specifically with the English teachers in those schools to develop language-teaching skills which would broaden their repertoire. Our trainers would work at classroom level in partnership with local teachers, supporting them in using new materials, planning lessons, developing new techniques and demoing lessons where required. This avoided a top-down model, and its success would be based on the establishment of professional and personal partnerships. Each trainer would tailor support to the needs of the teacher and pupils, building in the teacher's existing skills and adding others as required. By training teachers rather than teaching pupils we hoped to make the programme relatively sustainable. In addition, we would work with the larger NGOs active in the area, providing this specialist input into their wider programmes. By partnering with them, we would avoid overlap and duplication. This all sounded pretty doable, in theory. But in fluid and unpredictable situations, the road to hell is paved with well-intended theories.

One critical issue was mutual understanding. Some of the Burmese thought we were there to teach English and then go home. Teaching for a few months was pointless; something more sustainable was needed, and this required the training of local teachers. This was not always fully understood (or was perhaps deliberately misunderstood), and from time to time one of our team would roll up at a school to find that the teacher had not turned up, so would we stand in for the day? Or the school was short-staffed and the regular teacher was needed in other classes, so would we take a class for the day? It's also cheaper for a school to use a Western volunteer than pay a local teacher. Further to that, 'buy-in' by local staff was crucial. They had to want to do this, and there was a story running around that head teachers would take volunteers because they thought that volunteer placements were linked to funding. If a teacher was not interested in broadening their skills or the head did not really see any point in training, then support was pointless. In fact, the upshot of all of this was that our project could in many ways be counterproductive. That's a hard pill to swallow. But gradually we were getting the hang of it and came to expect these setbacks and misunderstandings and push on with the project, carefully and with an appreciation of the reality of the situation. Above all, recruitment of the right kind of trainer was required, and targeting the right kind of teachers and schools completed the equation. Working with untrained teachers took patience; sometimes it was two steps forward and one back. Building confidence was crucial and teachers would progress at their own pace. This took time, and building relationships became one of the most important elements of the programme.

We also had to take into consideration other NGOs, so we were very open with them about our plans and offered to work cooperatively. The American NGO World Education, under the leadership of Fred Ligon and Greg Antos, was excellent to work with and we put together a programme through which we could operate without duplicating any training, and in fact delivered a five-day training programme along with World Education staff. It was, after all, a pilot, and at the end of the three months we would take stock and prepare for the next phase. That's if we had any money.

We were quite secure in Mae Sot but elsewhere the border was volatile. I hadn't seen Dan for a while and the word was that he had gone on a bender. One morning Dan returned and his prodigality brought some tension into the usually balmy atmosphere of Coffee Corner. Dan had news. An unbelievably huge force of nine hundred Burmese and DKBA troops had crossed the border about thirty miles south at Umphang. I had heard about this incursion, and that schools had been burnt. Dan claimed that Karen villagers had fled across the border and been turned back by the Thai army. Some had been shot by the Burmese. Allegedly, the fighting was over control of the crops which were now ready to be harvested. The KNLA had pushed back the Burmese but there were still pockets of fighting, and a grain store had been burnt and a Thai captain killed.

Our three-month pilot was coming to a close and I was preparing to leave for England. I now knew that, with the idea of a mobile unit of trainers, we really had something special to build on. We had three excellent young trainers who had piloted the project, turning theory into practice. We knew we could make this work, but without funding we were going nowhere. However, sometimes life has plans of its own.

Riding home on my motorcycle through the ill-lit streets of Mae Sot, I recognised a figure in front of me on a bicycle. He stopped beside a coffee shop and I pulled up beside him, removed my helmet and said, "Do you remember me?" There was something of what is generally called a pregnant pause. The cyclist, a man of middle years in shorts and T-shirt, was a former trainer for MEP. A year or two previously he had volunteered for us for a relatively short time. He was a gifted teacher, but the relationship had been very difficult and had broken down fairly quickly. Before he disappeared, he had told me, "I am looking for something to believe in." After he'd left I'd received very little news about him, but had heard that he had found work in the Karen refugee camps. Our meeting that night was brief, cordial and cool, but we wished one another well. It was something of a closure, but there was to be a twist in the tale.

Three days later I was making my usual round of the schools on my motorcycle when I received a phone call from Fred Ligon at World Education. He informed me that he had just received the news that during the night the former volunteer whom I had met a few days previously had died in Nu Po refugee camp. I was shocked. He had apparently had a medical condition, leading to speculation that this had contributed to his sudden, unexpected death. For the rest of the day Fred and I were involved in making the required arrangements with the British Embassy following the death of a British national. Early the next morning I received a call from an old friend working in the camps. The news was astounding. Unknown to us, our volunteer had been well off and had left us a sizeable sum of money. The realisation that we could now build our programme almost anaesthetised me for the rest of the day. I wandered around, riven by a range of conflicting emotions as the relationship with our benefactor had been far from easy. Hopefully, at least, he had eventually found something to believe in.

As for me, well, I was now ready to sign up as a devotee of Shiva; in a manner of speaking, that is. One has to keep one's options open.

Moving On

2008–2009

During the next two years the money bequeathed to us funded a mobile trainer programme in the Burmese migrant schools of Mae Sot. The charity now deployed a team of six trainers, each allocated a cluster of four or five schools for a period of three months. It also now had the services of Clive Taylor, a former deputy director in the British Council network and projects manager for the Asia–Pacific area. This was a major step forward but there was still one crucial element missing. The charity could not provide Burmese teachers with internationally accredited certificates. We were soon to find a solution to this problem.

Eleven

Living on the Edge

**Colonel Moustache, Mad Dogs and Angels
Two Years Later,
Mae Sot, Thai–Burmese Border, 7 November
2010, the Day of the Burmese Elections**

Colonel Moustache had taken the town of Myawaddy, just inside Burma, and two rocket-propelled grenades had landed on the Thai side of the border. There were injuries. This was the news blurted out by a lady who, in something of a sweat, hurriedly parked her bike outside the Oasis Cafe at 10.30 one morning. Quickly finishing our coffee, Clive, our trainer Karen and I, took stock of the situation. We had a team of six working in the schools scattered along the Thai border. We had no idea of the scale of the fighting, nor if it would spread over the border from Myawaddy about five kilometres away. The lady cyclist added that thousands of refugees were fleeing across the river that formed the border. At times like this one fears the worst.

Quickly digested caffeine fuels disaster fantasies. I phoned the team, telling them to get back to Mae Sot immediately. One of them, James, could not be contacted as he had a new number. He would be in one of the outlying schools further up the Moei Valley; an isolated area accessible only by a narrow potholed road. At that point the river was shallow and a whole division could have crossed the border undetected. Eventually, through a string of phone calls, we tracked him down. It was his day off and he was at the municipal pool! I took off to the border to see for myself what was happening.

So who, then, was Colonel Moustache? In typical Burmese fashion he went by two names: Saw Lah Pwe and Bo Nat Khan Mway. He was head of the DKBA's 5th Brigade, the Golden Drum Brigade, and was commonly known by the English translation of his name, Bo (Colonel) Moustache, a reference to his magnificent facial furniture. The DKBA had broken away from the KNLA in 1994 and joined up with the Burmese military, the Tatmadaw. They had since been offered the role of a border guard force, with the right to collect taxes and conduct business. The story was that, due to some concerns about being disarmed, Bo Moustache had made it clear that he was against the proposal. Rumours and counter-rumours filled the bars and cafes and one never got to the bottom of it. Somehow this had all led to the attack on Myawaddy, which was controlled by the Burmese army. Now thousands of people were streaming across the border into Mae Sot. The border itself was the shallow Moei River, and most had waded across as the main Friendship Bridge was closed. Rumours circulated about a group stuck on a sandbar in the middle of the river, and their identity became clearer later in the day. Estimates ran at twenty thousand refugees. It's always the local people who just want to get on with their business who get caught up in these spats and head for the hills – or, in this case, the other side of the river.

Arriving at a field outside the Thai army barracks, I was stunned by what I saw. Thousands of people were sitting on the grass, some taking whatever shade there was under the huge plane trees on the perimeter, others crammed under an extensive awning as if they were attending some bizarre garden party. The Thai authorities had acted swiftly, and blue-and-yellow bell tents had been erected to offer shelter to some larger groups. Crowds directed by black-uniformed Thai border guards were still streaming through the gates of the barracks. Many were obviously in a state of shock and carrying whatever they had had time to scoop up. They were bewildered. Most were women, many with children, as the men had stayed behind to look after their property. I noticed a man staggering under the weight of a large case on his shoulder. Obviously, its contents were too valuable to leave. An old lady in traditional *tamein* (sarong) was supported by her grandson with denims and orange punk hair. A microcosm of Burmese social change, they were escorted into the compound by a border guard with an M16. The strain showed on the grandmother's face but, if nothing else, like almost everyone here, they had each other. One family had brought along their pet monkey dressed in a pink top and with a lead tied to its tail. It was proving to be a welcome diversion. A party of six adults dragging a string of fourteen young children carried a tower of rice flasks, and then a football team arrived, all still in the black-and-white strip of 'Great FC'. The ladies of the Red Cross were busy distributing food and water. Polystyrene containers full of rice and green beans were lined up. Contingents representing Islamic organisations and the Buddhist Sangha were doing their best to distribute packages of food and drink. A large lady remonstrated with a crush of children to get into some kind of line. At the perimeter, Thai soldiers guarded a mountain of bottles of water. At midday gunfire could still be heard in Myawaddy, but it died down as the afternoon wore on. The Burmese army had retaken the town.

One surprising casualty of the day was Phu's dog, a small red spaniel named Jimmy. For some odd reason Phu pronounced the name 'Jemmae', much like the Scots version. This seemed to automatically invite most Anglo-Saxons to mutter the Gaelic challenge 'See you, Jemmae' in some abomination of a Glasgow accent. Jimmy's main love was people, and people adored him. Phu had driven out to the refugee holding area in her truck to pick up a journalist. Jimmy tagged along for the ride but, excited by the sight of thousands of potentially loving people, jumped ship and disappeared into the crowd. In desperation Phu put out a description of the dog through a Thai captain. The thought of Thai soldiers moving through the mass of refugees calling 'Jemmae!' in a Clydeside accent is pushing the limits of the bizarre. Sadly, 'See You Jimmy' was never seen again; a victim of the power struggle. I reflected on the fate of the monkey with the pink top.

News came through about the group stuck on the sandbar. I was told that they were the families of the colonel's Karen fighters who had attacked the town. They were still on the sandbar, unwanted by the Thais and prevented from going back by the Burmese army. Colonel Moustache would not be pleased, but maybe he had a new, rather affectionate canine companion. I never did find out the fate of the lost souls on the sandbar.

And so, this was our life on the Thai–Burmese border: colourful, demanding, intriguing, frustrating, unpredictable and, at times, totally bizarre. For the team, in their terms, it was 'full on'. We now had a substantial project built around the concept of a mobile training unit. It was a simple and effective method of training teachers, and was relatively cheap. Reading about a system of teacher training sounds a rather dull undertaking but what we were doing was quite dynamic and is worthy of explanation. Each of our six teachers had a cluster of five or six schools and a Chinese bicycle with one gear and a very individual braking system. Every Friday afternoon they brought the English teachers from their cluster to a central point and delivered two hours of language and teacher training. The idea was to equip teachers with a range of skills to augment the basic rote learning. Teachers are teachers the world over, and if they think that new techniques don't work or are outside their capacity then the training manual goes in the bottom drawer. Well-meaning Westerners often turned up with detailed manuals that ended up in the head teacher's cupboard, to be brought out only to impress potential donors. So how, then, does one offer alternatives? The best way to convince teachers that these methods worked was for them to experience the techniques within their own learning and take their time to build confidence – in other words, to try the techniques and see if they worked for them.

So, our trainers set up language classes for the teachers and built in a variety of techniques. The week following the Friday session, the trainers visited each of their schools and worked with the teachers at classroom level. Language levels rose, confidence grew and teaching improved. It was never smooth as every teacher had their own problems and needs, but the trainer could tailor support accordingly. And skills learnt for English could be easily adapted to another foreign language and, with a bit of imagination, used for other subjects too. It was a simple and effective system whose success depended to a large degree on that key ingredient: good relationships. And for good relationships to flourish, you need people who can build them.

Among the six excellent volunteers we had at that time were three trainers who were to form the core of the team over the next three to four years and remain associated with the charity for some years to come. The most experienced was Karen Waterston from Edinburgh, a lady with huge expertise, boundless energy and infectious enthusiasm. Her energy was almost tangible; she would take on virtually any challenge, and loved training and building relationships with other teachers. However, she had one main concern about life in Mae Sot, which I will come to shortly. Katharine May, from Exeter, was something of a foil to Karen. Katharine was calm, quietly competent and had a natural authority. An engaging raconteur, she could hold us all with stories of her daily experiences with that key gift of a storyteller: the ability to see the extraordinary in the ordinary. She had one particular love, which I'll reveal shortly, which was central to Karen's concern about life in Mae Sot. The youngest was Linda Thomas from Hampshire. Known to us as Lindy Loo, she possessed a youthful innocence which hid an engaging eccentricity of character and personal warmth. She added a dash of butterfly colour to the dusty streets of Mae Sot, cycling in flowing daffodil-yellow and sometimes pink outfits. She was a source of endless stories and was loved by all. All three were blonde, attractive, and very good at what they did. They were known collectively and affectionately by other aid workers in the town as 'Bob's Angels'. I ignored this rather glamorous elevation but, secretly, felt some amused satisfaction. Our trio of young ladies was complemented by a tall, athletic young Irishman called John Cleary. John had a natural compassion tempered by an understated determination and resilience. He relished his work at the school on the Dump. He had taken to the 'Dumpers', and they to him. I couldn't endure more than twenty minutes at the Dump, with its flies, stench and poverty. John stuck it for three months. He later wrote about his experiences for the Irish press and donated the proceeds to the school. Looking back on all of this over many years, cynicism never clouds the fact that people are moved to do good for others in some of the most extraordinary of circumstances, and I've had the privilege of seeing this natural altruism time and time again.

To return to Karen's concern mentioned earlier. She had one pet hate and fear: street dogs. Her fears were not altogether unfounded. The street dogs lived in packs down alleys and on street corners, and could be quite formidable if in an aggressive mood, which was most of the time. They were mangy brutes, feral, focused on survival and totally fearless. They scavenged around the rubbish bins, mugged late-night shoppers coming out of 7-Eleven stores and, in packs, chased cyclists. Even the would-be mercenaries were wary of them. Apparently, there had been some experiment in microchipping them to monitor their whereabouts, but the dogs were cunning and beyond surveillance. There was a rumour that the Thais, being Buddhists, were averse to culling them, and so once in a while employed Muslims to thin out the packs. Urban myths abounded in Mae Sot.

Karen was borderline dogphobic. Apparently it was a 'family thing', and she became so worried about these creatures that she planned her routes to her schools to avoid risking an encounter and the inevitable pursuit. In doing so, she became something of an expert on the canine geography of the town, including the territories of whole packs of marauders and of lone predators. Such things can seriously affect the wellbeing of a team and the smooth functioning of a project. What, then, was the answer? Human ingenuity knows no bounds, and eventually, with almost military thoroughness, Karen dogproofed her bicycle. Black plastic bin bags stuffed full of newspapers were slung, like saddlebags, over the rear of the frame, preventing the dogs from snacking on her ankles. Armed with a pole, she faced the perils of the streets with the confidence of a Bengal Lancer. The dogs had met their match, and the project moved on.

Katharine, on the other hand, loved dogs, and they her. Growing up on a farm, she had acquired a natural affinity with animals. If anyone could have tamed the street dogs it would have been her. In fact, one entered her life in a serious way. A short-haired tan street dog turned up in her garden and, taking a liking to the place, decided to make it his base. Something of a celebrity, he went by the name of Toby and took up residence on Katharine's veranda. The two formed a bond. It's impossible to put a lead on a street dog. They live their own vibrant, adventurous lives, coming and going, eating and sleeping, fighting and fornicating. Toby became Katharine's companion and champion, and the team mascot. If Katharine went out at night, Toby would search the bars and cafes until he found her. He knew her routine and her favourite corners of the town. His affection was boundless, and if Katharine was dancing he wanted to join in, but this generally led to intimacy with her leg. Street dogs have no shame.

One of the favourite nightspots was the Aya bar and restaurant. This place was the ultimate in 'NGO cool'. At that time, Mae Sot was full of aid workers and volunteers from all over the world. The lingua franca in the NGO community was English, but the accents varied from clipped Home Counties through every European, Asian, North American and Antipodean version of the tongue. The vibe was friendly and tolerant and these dozens of (generally) young people enjoyed being part of an extended international family. A night out in Mae Sot was a much pleasanter experience than the hostile drunkenness that had taken over British town centres. George Orwell, writing about his Spanish Civil War experiences in *Homage to Catalonia*, said of his battalion of volunteers, 'there was not a bastard amongst them'. This was pretty much the case for the Mae Sot community. At Aya portraits of various 'resistance icons' covered the walls. Sitting Bull stared down impassively, Che Guevara struck a romantically heroic pose, Aung San Suu Kyi looked, as always, implacable. From time to time the bar took up pet causes. One that received much attention was freedom for women prisoners in Burma. A massive banner was created with a logo combining a Burmese Boudicca figure and a dove. This dominated the restaurant and intimidated the clientele for some time. It was a strange mixture of images beaten only by a trinity I came across in a small cafe in Mae La refugee camp, where posters of Christ and the Buddha were joined by one of Arsène Wenger, at that time the manager of Arsenal FC and, apparently, new Messiah. Aya's 'beat' atmosphere was heightened by its world music and blues soundtracks and a small library of what could be generally labelled 'protest literature', featuring autobiographies of political prisoners. The place was run by a team of former members of the All Burma Students' Democratic Front (ABSDF). This was a group of students who'd fled to the border area as a result of the crackdown following the 1988 uprising. They were generally young people from the city, and had joined up with the Karen, who'd armed and trained them. Some had now given up their M16s for guitars. One Friday night, Cho, a former ABSDF officer, now sporting a ponytail hanging over his denim jacket, thrashed out passionate songs on his guitar. It was quite a barrage in a relatively small area, so many of us preferred a seat by the door. Only Raymond, the hearing-impaired war photographer, sat beside Cho's amplifiers with a small, stunned entourage of Karen. At Aya, protest and politics always infused the atmosphere, and I spent many hours listening to Art, a Thai writer and member of the Student Federation of Thailand. His father had been a communist, and Art's political commentaries were fascinating and endless. Aya was a master stroke of marketing. There is a Burmese saying that a body has four rooms, each catering for a key aspect of being human: the mental, the physical, the emotional and the spiritual. To live fully you need to visit each of these rooms every day. At Aya you could do it in fifteen minutes.

Another watering hole of some character was the Bai Fern Restaurant. The setting was Thai Buddhist with something of the *Hofbräuhaus*. Beautifully carved wooden furniture filled a semi-open space, and the walls were covered with rather esoteric images of pools, trees, plants and monks, all slightly out of focus, giving a sense of Buddhist impermanence. The main drawback was the musical tastes of the rather more permanent owner, a balding German in his sixties with a penchant for Hawaiian shirts. His behaviour varied from the eccentric to the embarrassingly bizarre. Every night he would sit in the smokers' corner while diners enjoying their pad Thai noodles and red curry endured full-volume oompah-pah music from Munich punctuated by baroque ballads by Engelbert Humperdinck. Deep in his mental bierkeller the owner sat alone every night. He spoke German to his Thai diners and Burmese staff and me and seemed unfazed by our total lack of comprehension. His solace was the music and he would get upset when diners, suffering from profound culture shock, asked him to change the soundtrack to something more, perhaps, Thai. This always resulted in determined resistance. A Germanic cultural presence had to be maintained. An isolated and lonely figure, one can only wonder how he had become so at odds with the world and despite his 'eccentricities' had created a restaurant of great character and good food which remained one of my favourites in the town.

He also had a Thai stepson who, one night, appeared with what I took to be a young lady. 'She' was actually a gay cross-dresser wearing a flowing, patterned outfit. The Thais are very tolerant of what could be termed sexual fluidity. The stepson was a first-rate chef and, surprisingly, emotionally undamaged after years of beer-hall songs, had opened a restaurant called Charm, which, with its art nouveau Gustav Klimt murals, was the place to be seen – as long as you weren't wearing lederhosen.

Many restaurants employed Burmese staff on low wages. They were particularly vulnerable, and from time to time this led to ugly little scenes. For many Thai men the Burmese girls were fair game, and one night in a restaurant a young waitress came over to my table and asked if I could get her out of the place as she was being hassled by a drunk demanding sexual favours. The Thais are by international standards an intelligent and gentle people, but they get terribly drunk. She was ethnic Karen and lost. I couldn't do much, but a friend of mine could. Patrick Kearns had come out to the border some years previously and, with his own resources, established a progressive school in one of the camps. He followed this by setting up employment schemes for young people in the town, and was presented with an award from the Dalai Lama. He got this young lady a safer job. Over the years it was a privilege to meet ordinary people who had done such extraordinary things.

My favourite bolthole was a noodle stall with tables covered with plastic cloths advertising Coca-Cola. The stall, a mobile kitchen with a yellow fluorescent sign, was parked outside a karaoke and music bar and restaurant. I came to call it the Arts Centre. The stars of the show were resident singers supported by what appeared to be a struggling troop of sex workers. Thai men and the odd Burmese came and went, picking up their ladies for the night. One had something of a niche appeal. She was a quite ample woman approaching middle years who always dressed in the most peculiar and deceptive fashion: grey slacks, a white shirt with narrow black tie, and something approaching a tweed jacket. Whether she intended to create the impression of a schoolgirl or a civil servant was beyond me. I suppose much would depend on the fantasies of the client. There's just no accounting for taste. She became a nightly feature in the tragicomedy that played out under the yellow neon light. I was fascinated by these small but poignant dramas involving lives I could only imagine. But what I came to the noodle stall for was not the food, nor the 'cabaret', nor even the cool beer. It was something much more intoxicating.

The first step was getting there, and Toby was the key. At night, as a group, we would cycle home, which was quite an undertaking given the packs of dogs who were out to ambush anything. Households left their rubbish bags out in the streets for the refuse collections which took place during the night. However, first takers of the rubbish were the street dogs, and they policed their areas with almost suicidal savagery. Toby knew the score and ran ahead of us, clearing a way through the snarling packs to allow safe passage. Even Karen warmed to him. He actually became something of a canine icon, and the NGO community gave him his own Facebook page. I would then cycle on through the night until I saw the yellow neon of the noodle stall and heard Thai singing drifting through the darkness. I was drawn to this like a Greek sailor to a siren's call. The particular kind of music favoured was *Luk Tung* (child of the field). Dealing with the hardships of rural life, it had its own divas who went by names such as Rain and Grasshopper. They were generally pictured looking quite desolate, as if struggling with some hidden grief. You didn't need to understand the words to understand the meaning, as the songs had a seductive melancholy that would touch any human heart. I loved this space at the end of the day. Without asking, the lady at the noodle stall stuck a Singha beer in front of me. No one bothered me, not even the 'schoolgirl', and the *Luk Tung* warmed my heart and, dare I say, fed my own indulgent melancholy. At that time in Mae Sot, you could experience a whole world of emotions in three hundred yards and a night out.

In the day job, things were moving on. We had secured the services of an adviser in the form of Clive Taylor. Clive was in all respects a 'senior figure'. His kindly manner and courtesy carried echoes of the past from a different Britain. Now retired from his work with the British Council, he brought much professional experience with him, which would take us a step further in our development and provide a huge contribution to local teachers. However, one thing was missing. The teachers were putting in all of this time and effort and at the end had nothing marketable to show for it. Few of them had any recognised qualifications, and although a certificate from us saying that they had undergone a training course was well received, it had no clout. Clive suggested that it might just be possible for our Burmese teachers to sit English language exams provided by

Cambridge Assessment, a branch of Cambridge University. This sounded to be just what was needed. It would not be easy. We would be working with displaced people living in precarious circumstances with no ID and limited means to study, and we had no classroom and no examiners. This called for another 'Shiva moment', and sure enough, fortune came our way in the form of the most prestigious school in Thailand and the remarkable King Zero.

Twelve

Making History

King Zero, Nam-Jai and the Cassowary,
Mae Sot, Thai-Burmese Border, 19 March 2011,
Four Months Later

Win Tun sat silently eyeing the neatly laid-out pencils, eraser and red plastic sharpener in front of him. Two years previously he had escaped the Burmese police and certain imprisonment. Now he faced a greater ordeal: the Cambridge exams. Seated in two rows, the Burmese teachers waited for the papers to be distributed by three examiners from the prestigious Harrow International School in Bangkok. This was the culmination of three months' study, and provided a great opportunity. It was a first for the teachers, for Harrow and for us.

Mae Sot's first official Cambridge exams got under way at 9.30 on the morning of 19 March at the Wattana Resort, a very charming cluster of Thai-style buildings surrounding a small lake. The resort tried hard to induce a sense of rural calm with leaping carp, tame deer and a couple of smiling terracotta elephants. However, the star attraction was something rather unexpected. Near the main gate, a cassowary – a menacing, emu-like bird with a dangerous bony protrusion on its forehead – scratched around in a pen. I remembered from my time spent wandering the world in my youth that the hill tribes of New Guinea believed the cassowary to be a dark omen. That wasn't something I wanted to remember on a day like this.

The journey to the Wattana resort had, in fact, begun four months earlier. Actually, reaching this point was a small miracle brought about partly due to the wonderful Thai quality of *nam-jai*; literally, 'water from the heart', or compassion and generosity. We had been trying to find accredited exams which could be delivered to Burmese migrant teachers living on the Thai border, and we had an idea that we could deliver the Cambridge exams. But exams need examiners. We could deliver the course, but not examine our own students. This led to what was to become a highly effective partnership between us, a small NGO working in difficult conditions, and one of the most prestigious names in education globally: Harrow School.

Harrow, founded in England in 1572, has a string of alumni that cover the kaleidoscope of British history, including Lord Byron, Robert Peel, Winston Churchill and Jawaharlal Nehru. It's steeped in English tradition; archery was not dropped from the curriculum until 1771. A year's school fees for one boy were more than the annual turnover of our charity. However, their rather cryptic motto, 'The Faithful Dispensation of the Gifts of God', hints at a spiritual as well as a secular mission. We were clearly in Shiva country here. The popularity of an English public-school education had spread East, and Harrow now had branches in Beijing, Hong Kong, Shanghai and Bangkok. Amazingly, Harrow International School, Bangkok, was also a centre for Cambridge exams. We contacted them and, unexpectedly, wonderfully and with much *nam-jai*, they agreed to help and provide examiners. We now had a course, candidates and examiners. Or so we thought.

The rule is that all candidates must provide documentary evidence that they are who they say they are. Under normal circumstances this is not a problem, but the Thai–Burmese border does not deal in the 'normal'. Burmese migrant teachers often have no passport or anything approaching legal documentation. You may remember that many found themselves in jail for a day or two as 'illegals', suffering potential post-traumatic stress disorder due to overexposure to Thai game shows. This could have meant the end of our journey. Fortunately, ID cards were now being issued by the local Ministry of Education. This sounded like a breakthrough and a literal get-out-of-jail card for our migrant teachers. However, there was a twist: the exam rules required that ID cards display a photograph of the bearer. Our charity rules, based on hard experience, require us never to assume anything, so frantic phone calls were made to Simon Dickinson, a British contact at the Burmese Migrant Workers' Education Committee (BMWEC), who emailed us an ID card displaying, like a small icon, the required photograph. One would now assume that one was out of the woods and running clear, but assumptions were dangerous indulgences in Mae Sot. The exam was scheduled for 19 March and many Burmese teachers' ID cards ran out on the 1st and would not be reissued until the beginning of the school year in May. A sense of imminent disaster returned. Thankfully, the local Ministry of Education, with gallons of *nam-jai*, encouraged by some compassionate support from Simon and, I speculated, probably afraid of being accused of human rights violations for exposing jailed Burmese to Thai daytime TV, agreed to issue special IDs for our candidates covering the whole of March. Collective sighs of relief were almost seismic.

Other essentials for exams are 1) somewhere to teach the course, and 2) somewhere to hold the exam. We had two classes: an upper Preliminary English Test (PET) and a lower Key English Test (KET) involving, in total, twenty-three candidates. Suitable classroom space was not widely advertised but, hearing of our problems and responding with true Buddhist compassion and generosity, the day was saved by the intervention of King Zero of the remarkable Best Friend Library. So who was King Zero, and why did he have a library? The story is inspiring.

Best Friend was part of the resistance to the generals in Burma. It was an amazing organisation run by three monks: King Zero (apparently a reminder that the country actually still needed a good leader, and a metaphysical poke in the eye for the powerful generals), the erudite Ashin Sopaka, and Ashin Kovida, a former stand-up comedian who had taken the robe. The military junta regarded ideas as dangerous, and ideas are found in books. Aung San Suu Kyi's *Letters from Burma* was banned and other authors, such as George Orwell, regarded with suspicion. The generals' answer to thought control was equally Orwellian: licence the libraries and have spot checks. In response, in

1999 a group of Buddhist monks pooled their books and set up 'free libraries' in Burma without a licence. They called their organisation Best Friend. Its main belief is that education can open people's ears and eyes, and is a key way to eradicate poverty. At one point, Best Friend operated fifteen libraries and taught English, French, Japanese and Burmese. The libraries provided both monks and laypeople with access to uncensored information and literature, and served as meeting places where people could converse freely. One of Kovida's stock jokes was about a Burmese man who travelled to England for a dental appointment. When asked why he had come all that way when there were dentists in Burma, he replied, "Yes, there are plenty of dentists in Burma, but we just can't open our mouths!" The generals didn't like jokes against them and had locked up a couple of comedians called the Moustache Brothers who were into political satire. Kovida was wise to join the Sangha.

Then came the great uprising of the Buddhist Sangha in 2007. The Saffron Revolution, as it was called, saw thousands of monks take to the streets in protest against military rule. Monks are hugely respected in Burma, but the crackdown was brutal and King Zero, also known as Ashin Issariya, went into hiding. The military police pursued him for fourteen days, and if caught he says he would have been tortured. He evaded capture for over a year and, on 21 October 2008, eventually crossed the border and arrived in Mae Sot. His statement to Radio Free Asia was most revealing. "Before you start doing this kind of work, you have to be prepared to face extreme consequences, including the loss of your life. Otherwise, you cannot function," he said, and then, with deeply Buddhist allusions, added that the Burmese people "have been starved and choked of all the opportunities which can improve their lives. We have to liberate ourselves from the military dictatorship to be relieved from our suffering."[7] Ashin Sopaka spoke fluent English, was strikingly handsome, and did the PR work for the group. In his presence I noticed that our trainer, Karen, fell silent and still in a very focused and elemental kind of way. Secretly, Karen had something of a crush on Sopaka. This could have been food for a novel, perhaps even an opera, but Sopaka was devoted, for the moment, to the Dharma. However, this would not remain the case during the dreadful days to come. Following the military coup of 2021 Ashin Sopaka would renounce the monkhood and take up arms. As always with the Burmese, a transformation requires a new name, so instead of 'Sopaka' which is the Pali word for a 'waif or stray' he was now known as Bo Thanmani, 'Lieutenant Steel'. Using the alias he would lead a guerrilla unit of the People's Defence Force (PDF) in the fight against the Junta. In a way, his life stood as a metaphor for the dilemma that would face the whole of Burma when the storm eventually broke.

The three monks soon found themselves in exile in Thailand. In Mae Sot they opened up a Best Friend Library in a three-storey building in the Burmese Quarter just behind the colourful mayhem of the Burmese market. It had shelves of books in Burmese and English, and a black faux-leather three-piece suite. The ubiquitous posters of Aung San Suu Kyi, looking implacable as always, stared

---

7   Copyright RFA 2008.

down from the walls. Beside the entrance was a fish seller who received deliveries over the course of the day, giving a marine-like ambience to the downstairs rooms of Best Friend.

We'd got to know the monks and offered one of them a place on our Cambridge course. When we joked that it might be expensive, Sopaka replied, "How many books do you want?" They agreed to help us out by providing a space where we could deliver the course. We were offered a classroom with a view: the roof of the Best Friend Library. It was windy but we put up plastic windbreaks and purchased cheap desks and chairs. It was a venue of some character, with sounds from the market mingling with language drills involving the present perfect tense. Karen and Linda took to the work in earnest. A secure venue for the exam with holding areas for candidates was outside Best Friend's sphere of influence, but luckily, the East does not have a monopoly on *nam-jai*, and World Education stepped in with an offer of a room at the Wattana Resort. It made a perfect venue, even with the cassowary.

Under 'normal' circumstances one could assume that the picture was almost complete. A couple of times a week, the candidates would travel to the Best Friend Library for classes. But, as discussed above, in this environment assumptions are dangerous. Some candidates lived out of town and had to travel at night. They felt uncomfortable about this as, even though they had ID cards, the local constabulary could be difficult. A couple of days in jail suffering a forced diet of mind-numbing Thai game shows would destroy all knowledge of the English language. Transport became an issue. However, with the help of World

Education a vehicle was hired to do the run on Thursday nights and Saturday mornings. And so, after three months of lessons on the roof of the Best Friend Library and nocturnal drives avoiding the attention of the gendarmerie, Win Tun et al. were ready for the exam.

The day before the exam was (in some respects for us all, although we didn't realise it at the time) a day filled with destiny. We had never met the examiners from Harrow International School, Bangkok, and found the school's formidable reputation rather intimidating. They had given up their weekend to conduct the exam for free, and the school would pay the exam fees for the candidates. This was *nam-jai* of epic proportions. Clive and I waited nervously at the airport for the team to arrive, and then, through the trickle of arrivals, came our destiny in the shape of David Eastgate, Dava Romyanond and Wendy Gordon. David, from Norfolk, was Harrow's exams officer; Dava, in addition to examining candidates, provided the Thai element so crucial for much of the organisation; and Wendy, a New Zealander, was the experienced second examiner. I suspect they were as nervous as we were.

The following day, the day of the exam, started badly with a 'cassowary moment'. Getting twenty-three teachers who lived in scattered communities around Mae Sot to a central point at a given time was a logistical nightmare. However, everything had been organised with almost military precision. A *song-tau*[8] would pick up the candidates at certain points, at given times. This had been thoroughly rehearsed with all concerned and we felt certain

---

8   A converted pickup truck.

all was ready. But on the Thai border, certainty is even more dangerous than assumption. Never allow yourself to be lulled into a false sense of security in this part of the world. Never believe that anything will happen until it really happens. Duly, the *song-tau* did not arrive at 7.30 a.m. as planned but was, in fact, forty miles south of Mae Sot in a remote village. Reasons given were vague even for an area where vagueness seems like certainty. But at the eleventh hour the day was saved by Phu from Coffee Corner who, overflowing with *nam-jai*, gave us the use of a very smart four-wheel drive, and panic and disaster were avoided. The exams got under way as planned and the rest of the day ran like clockwork. At four o'clock, after a nerve-racking day, Karen and Linda hugged and high-fived their students. David from Harrow said he had never seen so many smiles on an exam day.

Looking back, I cannot help but marvel at this moment. David, Dava and Wendy became our colleagues and then our friends. Harrow, Bangkok, as I will explain, became a partner in our work, and this partnership affected the lives of thousands of Burmese teachers, over five hundred of whom, at the time of writing, have gained Cambridge certificates. We were able to extend the project into the border refugee camps, to the monastic schools of southern Burma, and even into the internally displaced persons' (IDP) camps of war-torn Kachin State. It also led to international recognition for our work, which I shall explain later.

And what of the cassowary? Thwarted, it brooded darkly by the gate and waited for next year.

Taking Stock

For Those Who Wish to Go Down This Path

Don't go charging off down the first road you see. There will be many requests for support; most genuine, but some bogus. Some will lead to a dead end. Take your time and look around until the way becomes clear.

Get a good grasp of the situation and then develop a sound, simple idea on which to build your organisation. Keep in mind that it's not what you want but what people need. This is the key. It will attract like-minded people as well as funding. You will need both. You can then begin to build your team for the longer term.

Find your niche. Don't duplicate or overlap. Work to complement what other NGOs and similar organisations do. Partnerships and relationships are important within your organisation and without. Make sure you have people in your team who can build and maintain such. Make this part of your ethos.

Create an attractive identity for the organisation and for

your team. People will then take pride in being part of it. Build a role for everyone and value all.

You'll always run into cynics but don't let them discourage you. You can't change the world, but do whatever you can and add your light to the sum of light. But do check why your light is burning in the first place and don't forget that you are a human being.

And don't sing 'Kumbaya'.

Moving On

2011

In 2011 MEP took a major step in our development by becoming involved in one of the biggest projects we ever faced. The large Dutch NGO Zoudoost Azië Refugee Care (ZOA) had been delivering teacher training in the Karen refugee camps for some years. The Karen required the development and delivery of a new English language course, and made a request to us. We agreed to offer this in partnership with ZOA. For us this was something of a milestone as it was our first formal partnership with a well-established international NGO, and came with an office which would give us a valuable base for our work. All we needed was a team including teachers skilled in writing textbooks as well as delivering training.

The task was huge. It would take several years to complete the programme, which would cover the texts and training needed for Grades 1 to 6 – that is, children from five years old to about eleven. There were roughly eighteen thousand such children across seven camps. We would focus initially on the largest camp, Mae La, with a population of around forty thousand. The camp was about fifty kilometres north of Mae Sot, and would require a daily journey of about one and a half hours each way. This was a volatile border, and our team would have to pass through a number of checkpoints manned by black-uniformed Thai border guards. There were twenty-seven primary schools in the camp, with an unknown number of teachers of English. The camp itself was a vast maze of bamboo houses spread along two miles of the border. There were no maps, and the actual locations of the schools were vague. We would have to deliver this project in the dust of the dry season and through the monsoon.

The task of designing the project fell to Katharine May, whom you met earlier. Initially she was supported by John Cleary who had been working at Sky Blue, the 'Dump School'. John, like Katharine, was rarely fazed by anything. Later he would make *Crossing the River*, a successful documentary about the situation, which was shown at the Open City Documentary Film Festival. ZOA provided an experienced trainer in the form of Alice Harwood from Uganda. Together they came up with a plan which is worth sharing as it gives some idea of the difficulties our teams faced over the coming years, and may even provide a useful model for anyone going down this path in similar circumstances. Please see the Appendix for details.

Thirteen

Offering Not Giving

The Sphinx, a Bamboo Riddle and Designer Kitchens, Mae La Refugee Camp Thai–Burmese Border, September 2011

The checkpoint was the signal for the team members to stir themselves from their chat, snooze, daydream or the music from their headphones, and get their backpacks ready to jump out at whichever gate they needed to that day.

Mae La camp coming into view never failed to make an impression. The misty valley with thousands of bamboo homes built into the hillside, and what it all meant, created a sense of heightened anticipation which was renewed every day. Stretching for about two miles along the road, Mae La sheltered under a limestone escarpment which, with a little imagination, was almost Sphinx-like in shape. The camp had its riddles too, both human and otherwise. The team was equipped with rudimentary maps offering a vague idea of where in the bamboo maze their schools might be located. The closer you got, the more the camp came to life: trucks, people, deliveries, animals, smoke rising, voices, schoolchildren and, of course, the shelter at each gate for the Thai guards, reminding everyone that Mae La is not an ordinary village. There are rules.

The camp had in fact been relocated following a 1998 attack on the original camp at Huay Kaloke, when soldiers from the Burmese-allied DKBA entered in a jeep and on motorbikes and burnt and mortared the densely inhabited camp. The dry bamboo houses almost exploded in the heat. The Sphinx now watched over Mae La's forty thousand occupants in more secure circumstances. Katharine, the team leader, describes the feelings of our team as they approached the camp:

> *The mood in the truck was usually positive – the promise of another day – and we at least began the day clean! We sometimes had to brace ourselves for the heat, or the cold, or the rain, and usually held our breath slightly as we walked past the guard and through the gate, in case today was one of the days when our passes would be questioned, or there was a new guard, unfamiliar with our faces and suspicious of our motives for entering the camp. Sometimes we felt tired in anticipation of the trek we had not yet begun, but it always got easier once we were under way. Sometimes we were determined to have a better/ more productive day than the one before; sometimes pessimistic because things hadn't been going so well. Sometimes, if it had been a particularly rip-roaring*

*ride to get there, we were just relieved to have arrived
in one piece.*

The first team MEP sent into Mae La comprised three
English language teachers – Caroline Milne, a former
department head from Bishop Auckland; Laura Gibbs
from London, who had experience with refugees; and Sam
Weekes, a specialist in materials design from Bristol – with
Katharine as their leader. It was a skilled group with much
energy and enthusiasm, which they needed in order to not
be daunted by the task they faced. Katharine continues:

*But nothing will compare to our first day in the camp
as a new team. The weather was shocking. There had
been landslides and floods, and the rain showed no
signs of easing up. We were all very nervous, firstly
about finding our way to each school, then about
meeting each teacher and their class, and then about
finding our way back out. We all felt awkward; not
only the usual awkwardness of a first day in a new
job, but also physically awkward as we skidded and
tripped and sweated our way around, making much
harder going of it than the residents.*

Physically, this was a challenge. The camp climbed
the slopes of the Sphinx, with the only access to the
communities on the higher ridges being via slippery,
muddy paths which turned into streams in the rain, or in
the dry season became dangerous as the loose shale gave
no grip. Occasionally, a greasy concrete path rose almost
sheer from the main valley. Duck-foot, a method perfected

by the Karen, was the best way to avoid a fall in flip-flops. In the camps it was the small wounds that could prove nasty. Falls were frequent and could result in skinned feet and hands which could quickly become infected. Buildings were on a Karen scale, and loftier Western heads were bruised and bloody after collisions with low beams or sharp bamboo eaves. To negotiate the camp, our team had to identify landmarks. The white stupa of a Buddhist temple could be an orientation point from a distance, but these quickly disappeared in the mass of bamboo houses, so shops, small cafes, bamboo bridges, signs providing information on sanitation, education or personal security – in fact, anything of note acted as guides. Katharine and the team were thrown into a new and confusing world that would have fazed even the Sphinx. But for Katharine the responsibility had so many aspects:

I personally felt a huge amount of responsibility for the team, whom I had sent off in ponchos with a photo of a hand-drawn map and patchy (at best) phone reception; that they felt supported, enjoyed themselves, and were at their pickup spot at the end of the day and willing to come back the following day.

This project was a first for us, and the responsibility was quite onerous for the team. They wanted to prove to ZOA that we could do this, and, importantly, we had to get the local teachers on board. And here was the rub. One of the key lessons that we learnt while working with the Burmese was very simple: if the people you are working with do not buy into the project, then it will never really succeed. This seems obvious but is often overlooked in your almost evangelical desire to do what you think is self-evidently correct. The spirit in which something is done is as important as the content of the project. Generosity is one of the critical elements in what is broadly called 'aid work'. In Buddhist societies it is held as one of the prime virtues, and it is fundamental to our sense of our own humanity. But generosity is associated with giving, and giving can come with problems. You can't always guarantee that the recipient is grateful, nor that they really want your gift. It may well be accepted and even appreciated but there can be a residual, underlying sense of grudging humility and indebtedness. This is an especially sensitive area in intercultural exchanges involving a disadvantaged group. If possible, offering is a better option, followed by the development of ownership and empowerment by the recipient. Katharine's team had to gain the trust and respect of the local teachers and offer them a stake in it all. So, every Friday afternoon they took their groups through the new materials, introducing and demonstrating new teaching techniques, and the teachers learnt about the techniques by trying them out themselves and then on their pupils, modifying them as necessary. The following week our team followed up by offering in-class support. Step by step, this creates confidence, ownership and buy-in. Katharine explains the initial difficulties:

> *In most cases, my relationship with each teacher started out fairly uneven and a little awkward. They wanted me to do most of the teaching. They preferred to watch, which was entirely understandable, until they felt more sure of what they were being asked to do. But they also liked to carry my bags; get me a*

chair, a drink and a snack; or even position a fan so that it was blowing in my red face! This was all part of their hospitality, but rather than put me at ease, it made it harder to connect with them as colleagues, not that I would ever have said anything. However, this improved with time, and some quickly took to the idea of partnering, while others needed more time. The Friday sessions really helped with this as teachers were able to see me in a different light; see others progressing and gaining confidence, enough to start modelling and demonstrating activities themselves. The more time I spent with each teacher, and the more time we spent planning outside of class, the more it helped us get through this initial barrier.

I was always an outsider, but over time I began to feel less like a visitor. I had my spot in the camp education office. Heads did not turn whenever I arrived at schools. I carried my own bags, and it really felt like we were a close-knit group of teachers working together. Fridays were a joy. We worked hard, but there was always a lot of energy and laughter, fruit and 3-in-1 coffee.

So, who were these teachers to whom we offered this training, and how did they respond? Again, I have to turn to Katharine for this first-hand experience. A picture emerges of human beings facing often complex problems and an uncertain future:

I did not learn in great detail each teacher's story. If they did not offer it, I did not ask. Most of the teachers I worked with were between twenty and forty. Many – girls in their early thirties, like me – had arrived in the camp when they were in high school. It seemed that their parents had experienced the very worst horrors when the teachers were young children. I frequently heard of Karen villages and homes being destroyed, burnt, or made unsafe due to Burmese army occupation or landmines. Many families had lost everything in terms of land and possessions when they had fled, and, ceasefire or not, they were too afraid to return. Some of the brutal effects of landmines were visible among the population. Landmine training was among the many NGO training days/workshops.

LB, a Karen teacher around my age, was an English teacher in one of our pilot schools. She was barely there in the first term, and rarely attended Friday sessions. When I met her, she was extremely timid and struggled to make eye contact. Soon into the project, I was repeatedly told that she was off sick, but she seemed to attend other days. I was often left to teach her classes by myself, and began to worry that she was avoiding being involved. For a teacher to stop teaching because of our involvement would be the worst possible outcome. There was clearly something going on. I managed to have some time with her and do some planning with just her, and she slowly began to get more involved. I later found out that she had had a miscarriage (not her first) and was suffering badly with her mental health. Her husband came and went and eventually resettled in the US.

Once feeling better, she became a key member of the group and one of the more confident teachers. She'd rally the others, scold them for being late, and it was clear that she was a strong, capable and determined woman and teacher. Her husband was able to send her money and visit each year. She was waiting to join him. I spent time in her home in Mae La, with her mother, sister and dogs. I had to walk past their home to get to a few of my schools, and was often beckoned in for a quick drink or just a moment in the shade. When I left, both LB and I were pregnant, and our daughters were born just weeks apart. We keep in touch. She now lives in the US with her husband. She no longer teaches.

Another teacher, A, became a great friend. She was bright, had a wicked and naughty sense of humour, and was a natural and charismatic teacher and member of the group. Originally from Yangon, she was a chemistry graduate, and had the best English of the teachers. She was a Muslim single mother, again around my age, and lived with her nine-year-old son in the camp. I am not a hundred per cent sure how she ended up in Mae La, but she had an aunt and an older brother she was very close to who were also there. Piecing together our conversations, she had run away from her husband, and did not have the support of her parents. She suddenly disappeared at one point, which was really unsettling for the group. Ushering me out of the school, her head teacher simply told me that A had gone and her class was cancelled. A few days later

A's brother found me and said she'd gone back to Burma, but he couldn't say when or if she'd be back. It was not unheard of for people to suddenly move on, but this seemed so out of character. After a few weeks she reappeared, saying that she'd had to visit a sick relative but everything was fine now, and on we went.

She had a slightly different relationship with the other teachers. They were clearly fond of her and were impressed by her confidence and the twinkle in her eye, but they were not part of the same community, and their different ethnic backgrounds meant that they socialised less outside of the project. Inside, A was front and centre, particularly in our Friday sessions, and I could tell that she really enjoyed that. So much so that, as we moved from Grade 1 to Grade 2, so did she, and then again to Grade 3. This was not the plan. We were supposed to move with the children but work with different teachers along the way. The school, however, insisted that there was no other teacher for the job.

There were forty or more students in each class at A's primary school, with four classes all in one big barn-type building. The noise was tremendous. Most of the teachers carried canes. A did not. She was often in charge of two classes at once, and would dart between them, writing on the different blackboards. She was one of those rare teachers who are warm and put their students at ease, while keeping their attention and respect at all times. I loved watching her teach because, even though she didn't prepare as much as some of the others, she was such a natural.

We still have some contact, and after leaving I heard that she had got a job with a legal team, advising camp residents on legal matters. She said she might become a lawyer. I don't think she ever intended to be a teacher permanently, which was a great shame for the children, but I could see she had other ambitions.

Training teachers is never easy even in more favourable circumstances. In every case the dynamics between the trainer and the teacher, and the teacher and the class, are different, and each class is different. So, good teachers adapt techniques accordingly. Layered on top of this in the camps were cultural considerations. Teachers in Asian communities are greatly respected; part of a cultural hierarchy that includes older people, monks, holders of office, and anyone with an education. 'Keeping face' is crucial. Nobody wants to lose face, or do things that create circumstances in which others lose face. Teachers are not there to be questioned, and teaching is often considered akin to telling. To a certain extent this cultural model stands at odds with the Western emphasis on interrogation of fact and opinion and the social dynamic that education brings. All cultures contain paradoxes, and Burmese culture is no exception. The contradiction here is that Buddhism does not encourage blind acceptance and belief, but takes a very practical approach. Followers of the Dharma (the Buddhist path) are encouraged to listen to a teaching and then try it out to see if it works for them emotionally, spiritually or even physically. However, at the same time, while testing the veracity of beliefs, followers of the Dharma need a teacher, a guru, an experienced guide. This person is held in some esteem. I always wondered why the spirit of this empirical approach had not fully entered mainstream education even though respect for the teacher/guide certainly had. Katharine found that:

It was difficult for the teachers to accept making mistakes, but essential so that they would allow their students to do the same. Fridays were a safe time to almost rehearse the activities and lessons for the following week, right down to the pronunciation of vocabulary. Over time, rather than just reproduce the activities as we had practised them, some teachers were able to lift the techniques and apply them where needed. Not all could do this, and some needed more prescriptive guidance. Like with any job involving humans, we had to keep in mind that the teachers had a lot else going on in their lives, or on their minds.

And they certainly did have something on their minds, and that was getting out of the camp.

Near the main gate sat a most peculiar building. It looked like a showroom for a company specialising in kitchen design. In a refugee camp comprised of bamboo buildings, this was more than incongruous. Visible through a picture window in a brutalist concrete block sat an image of the West in the form of white goods – fridge, cooker, microwave, dishwasher – surrounded by glossy white benchtops and cupboards. This was the First World, this was 'lifestyle', this was aspiration. In particular, it was the USA, but it seemed as if it had just arrived from outer space.

It was all part of a resettlement programme taking refugees from the camp to third countries. The USA was popular, but Britain, Australia and the Scandinavian countries were prominently involved too. Resettlement was the choice of many as rumours abounded of Chinese companies taking their land in Burma, or of areas made unsafe by landmines. There were also stories of abuse of the system as the programme drew people into the camps and they did whatever they could to get their names near the top of the resettlement list. Every few weeks trucks packed with Karen hoping for a better life (and a nice kitchen) in Sydney, Sheffield or Stavanger rumbled out of the camp. Some remained together but sometimes families were dispersed all over the world. Still, those who didn't get a place in the trucks were often despondent at seeing their dreams shattered. Years later I met many who had been resettled in England. It was a mixed picture. Most had done it for their children, and tried hard to keep the Karen traditions alive while living in the bleak industrial terraces of Sheffield. I could never conceive of the scale of the sacrifice.

Others decided on a different route to a better life. There were fixers who, for a price including a cut for the police, would get you to a 'job' in Bangkok. One of our teachers saved up enough money for the cheaper route to the Thai capital. This involved trekking for days to avoid the checkpoints, and then being picked up and taken to Bangkok. She was told that she was guaranteed a job, but what kind of job it would turn out to be was open to speculation. She also had to pay for accommodation and the rest of the transport costs out of her wages. The sex trade and sweatshops fed on this kind of arrangement. But desperate people will do desperate things, and for some taking the risk seemed better than staying in the camp indefinitely. We never did find out what happened to this young lady. Perhaps she reconsidered.

It took Katharine and subsequent teams another four years to finish the project. Dozens of teachers were trained; textbooks studied, at any given time, by potentially about eighteen thousand children; and something that was hopefully sustainable was put in place. One key aspect that had to be kept in mind was that a lot of the (generally young) people whom we were training had not chosen teaching as their career. They were doing it as it was the best way to help make ends meet in a difficult situation, and this, along with the comings and goings in a refugee camp, naturally created a turnover of teachers. Our answer was to create a cadre of advanced skills teachers (ASTs) from the more experienced teachers who were in this for the longer term. They acted as trainers and mentors for new teachers coming into the schools. In these precarious situations nothing is perfect, but you offer whatever you can. Kitchen designers are especially welcome.

Moving On

Refugees fleeing the fighting inside Karen State were one of the main communities found on the Thai–Burmese border. They were confined to seven camps and, as Thailand was not a signatory to the UN Refugee Convention, not strictly 'refugees' in the legal sense, and the camps were regarded as 'temporary shelters'.

Outside the camps, however, a huge number of Burmese 'migrants' lived, at best semi-legally and often semi-permanently. They worked in the paddy fields, the sweatshops and, as mentioned earlier, the municipal rubbish dumps. Working in these precarious circumstances were some extraordinary individuals, but sometimes things were not quite as they seemed.

Fourteen

The Face of History

Moonlit Faces, Extraordinary Encounters and a Trust Betrayed
Mae Sot and the Moei Valley,
Thai–Burmese border

All things are the primal void,
Which is not born or destroyed;
Nor is it stained or pure,
Nor does it wax or wane.
(The Heart Sutra)

Almond eyes filled with curiosity and a little apprehension stared out over cheeks displaying what appeared to be full moons. The lunar effect was created by covering each cheek in a large disc of *thanaka*, a thick yellow paste made from the bark of a tree. Each disc revealed the rhythmic circular movement of the fingers with which it had been applied to the light brown skin. The moonlit face was striking; a face which carried the flow of history and of life itself.

The first time I saw such faces was amongst the young ladies of the NLD standing cheerfully outside the gate of Aung San Suu Kyi's house so many years ago in Yangon. Their smiles had linked one moonlit cheek to another. *Thanaka* was to be seen in every city, village and street in Burma. In practical terms the circles of paste protected the skin, but in the East circles take on a deeper significance. Here the rhythms of history are seen as cyclical; not a linear thrust as perceived in the West, but a constant cycle of change, death and rebirth. Nothing is permanent, all is in a state of flux, all is subject to the karmic laws of cause and effect. Our lives follow the same pattern. Caught on the Wheel of Life, haunted by our own sense of *dukka* (that life is never quite satisfactory), we move through the full gambit of human emotions, searching for wholeness which comes to us only fleetingly. This is the Dharma; the way things are. Importantly, in the Buddhist tradition the moon is of special significance. It represents the *bodhicitta*, the enlightened mind; a mind that strives towards awareness, wisdom and compassion. Knowing this lends a rather different interpretation to a face painted with moon discs.

In the Moei Valley dividing Thailand from Burma, mornings for me held much promise. In the freshness of the dawn, chants float from the Buddhist temples, welcoming the growing light. The Pali verses resound deeply in the throats of the monks as they have for over two thousand years, and their compelling rhythm and message set the pattern for the day:

Buddham saranam gacchami.
Dhamman saranam gacchami.
Sangham saranam gacchami.

To the Buddha I go for refuge.
To the Dharma I go for refuge.
To the Sangha I go for refuge.

The brief evenings, too, have their charm. In the sweep of the Moei Valley the greens are more verdant and the blues of the distant mountains inside Burma hold such deep allure. I loved motorcycling through the valley towards the end of the day to catch that special brief moment when the sun began to set and the boom of the temple bells echoed across the rice paddies dappled in the fading light, and when the red earth took on a deeper hue. Images linger: a goatherd in a conical bamboo hat and blue homespun tunic, sitting silently with his flock; tattooed monks in saffron robes filing past white stupas; the last light catching the golden pinnacle of a temple; a nun holding her hands in reverence towards the deep red circle of the setting sun. And at the point when one wishes these haunting images and the deep sense of peace they bring would last, they slip away as the brief light of evening with its heightened sense of reality succumbs to the inevitable darkness.

The cycles of history had rolled through the Moei Valley. The same sunset had witnessed the armies of Burma, Thailand and Japan come and go across the mountains, filled with lofty ambitions and deep fears, seeking glory, conquest or safety. They too marched to the Wheel of Life. MEP had adopted one such figure from history as a kind of emblem. This was the Thai Karen general Paw Waw. He had opposed the Burmese invaders at the end of the eighteenth century and made a last stand on the pass at what is now called Magic Mountain, just outside Mae Sot. He and his command were all killed, but the spirit of Paw Waw lingered. A huge red-and-gold figure of the general in full armour sits imposingly in a shrine built on the spot where it is claimed he made his last stand. Passing drivers blow their horns to show respect, and in the hope of acquiring good luck on their travels. The cave where Paw Waw's pregnant wife hid for safety is still a place of pilgrimage. His likeness with its tall conical helmet and spear appears on the sides of ambulances at the local hospital, and visitors to his shrine can purchase copper medallions bearing his image. The medallions were used as *deun tang plod pai* (safe travel) charms rather like St Christopher medals, and as this seemed appropriate to the kind of work we were doing with mobile units of trainers, we gave them to our teams and to anyone who helped us. In the circumstances, if of questionable efficacy, they proved very popular. And we are all to a greater or lesser extent caught in the sweeps and cycles of history. Some play a major role and become iconic figures, like Paw Waw. Others lead obscure lives but play almost incredible roles in shaping the destiny of others, and they too are Paw Waws in their own right. They will never get a shrine built in their memory, but they deserve the medallion at least. And there were many such people in Mae Sot.

One day, sitting in the shelter outside Hle Beh migrant school, I was joined by a lady of middle years wearing a dark Burmese dress, with hair swept back in the traditional style and her cheeks covered in *thanaka* moons. She told me in fluent English that she had been the chair of the NLD's women's section, the Mergui Division, and several years ago had fled Burma after being involved in a demonstration which had led to trouble from her employers. She now made a meagre living as a teacher at Hle Beh. In 2007, following the Saffron Revolution, her husband had been jailed. She said quite emphatically that she was very happy about this, and proud of him and of Aung San Suu Kyi. It didn't matter if Suu Kyi was in jail or not; she was still the head of the NLD and would lead the party in the elections and build democracy step by step. Rather thoughtlessly, I mentioned that I had been away from England for about five weeks and my wife didn't like me being away for that long. Matter-of-factly, the lady retorted that she hadn't seen her husband for five years. The response was sobering and threw my limp statement into perspective. I sat for a moment, rather embarrassed, and then was rescued when an old acquaintance arrived at the school and, seeing me, shouted across, "Is that Bob Anderson?"

With that, the lady, whom I had assumed to be Burmese, looked at me with surprise and, with a moon-linking smile, said, "Anderson – your name is Anderson? In that case, maybe we are related. My name is Dianne Anderson." Her father was Australian, her mother Spanish, and she had been brought up in Burma. I speculated that maybe her Australian family had originally come from Newcastle. Dianne left me with a sense of the complexities and nuances of history, and of her commitment and resolve. If people were prepared to sacrifice their lives and hold true to a cause, then perhaps the days of the military junta were numbered. She would have been a formidable chair of the Mergui, or even the Women's Institute in Gateshead.

However, Dianne was not alone. Equally impressive was Htet Htet Aung, the head teacher of a migrant school. She was sixty years old, single, and ran her school with quiet efficiency and compassion. The school was essentially a series of screened-off 'rooms'. During the monsoon the pounding of the torrential rains, magnified into a roar by the corrugated-iron roof, mixed with the staccato chanting of the classes, provided visitors with a rather heightened audiovisual experience. The one pleasure the rain afforded was that it dampened down the concrete dust which, in the dry season, rose from the walls and floor, hung irritatingly in the air, settled slyly on surfaces and invaded your food. Htet Htet Aung had a bare one-roomed house, with the most basic facilities, beside the school. Nevertheless, she was always crisply turned out in the Burmese style. With blue *temain,*[9] tight-fitting grey jacket, raven hair swept back, and *thanaka* moon face, she was ready to face the world with dignity. Why, then, was this genteel and elegant lady enduring such hardship? Sitting in her house with the rain thrashing the precarious corrugated-iron roof, she told me, "I have friends who go to Singapore and make a lot of money. They go back to Myanmar and buy a house. They say to me, 'You work with the migrants and come back to Burma with nothing.'" Htet Htet Aung paused to consider the content and linguistic complexities of her next English sentence, then continued, giving weight to each word, "I tell them I have everything. In my life I can help all of

---

9   A ladies' sarong.

these children." Another pause was followed by a statement which betrayed a wider vision. "And these children can help to build democracy." The metallic crash of the rain seemed to signal its approval. Conversations like this, and I had many of them, always left me sitting in silence, struggling with a vague sense of my own inadequacy. Htet Htet Aung was a lady of great dignity and quiet determination. It was a trait I much admired in the Burmese people in general; a quality that had seen them through so many difficulties in the past and, as it turned out, one they would need to draw on in the dark times that lay ahead for the nation.

Appearances are also deceptive. Htin Htin Mar was a slight, young Burmese lady who, on first meeting, seemed somewhat shy and a little hesitant. She was head teacher of the poetically named Irrawaddy Flower Garden Learning Centre and, wearing her dark hair long over her regulation white teacher's blouse, spoke quietly through a smile. Her staff were mainly cheerful, able young ladies who, with their moonlit *thanakaed* faces, giggled to hide embarrassment, and charmed all visitors. This was totally disarming and totally deceptive. The glint in Htin Htin Mar's eye betrayed a deeper truth. She ran the Irrawaddy Flower Garden with an authority, firmness and capability the military junta would have envied. The one drawback was that the route to the school was targeted by child traffickers. Htin Htin Mar and her staff were having none of this. Keeping an eye out for the would-be traffickers, they 'rode shotgun' on the *song-taus* which transported the pupils to and from school. Staff policed the boundaries, and signs had gone up: 'No photography. Visitors, please wait at the entrance'. This was stern stuff and provided a clear warning to traffickers of the vigilance of Htin Htin Mar and her team. This made the Flower Garden a popular school among parents. Htin Htin Mar and Karen became great friends, and we used the school as a training centre for teachers from the area and took some of them through the prized Cambridge exams. One day, in gratitude for our work with the teachers, I was invited to a meeting in the school hall. The hall actually comprised the totality of the school as there were no classrooms, not even partitions, just groups of desks clustered around blackboards, one group per grade. Sitting in the hall were rows of parents: farmworkers, labourers, market porters, washerwomen; the sunburnt, worn faces of those who struggle for survival on a daily basis. But I remember their bright eyes as they smiled and clapped when Htin Htin Mar presented me with a large basket of goods: tins of milk, packets of sweets, biscuits and 3-in-1 coffee sachets. The whole harp-shaped ensemble was neatly wrapped in cellophane. Receiving such from the poorest of the poor, the wretched of the earth, invites hollow cliches and defies meaningful description other than a sense of justice confounded.

Htin Htin Mar also had an interesting extracurricular skill. She could play football. 'Play', however, is a rather lukewarm verb in this case; it suggests rules and order and a competitive but sporting attitude. For Htin Htin Mar football was something bordering on a blood sport. Karen had set up a ladies' team, with Htin Htin Mar, naturally and unassailably, as captain. Although petite in the Burmese style, she took no prisoners and played on the sun-baked earth pitch with a lethal gamesmanship that made rules rather surplus to requirements, and had earned the nickname Bites-Your-Ankles. Given a year or so, it wouldn't have surprised me if she had been picked as centre half for Uruguay.

But the moonlit face that I shall never forget belonged to a rather stocky lady of middle years with a swinging ponytail and only half a mouthful of teeth. This was Pan. She was a street vendor, a cleaner, and much more. She toured the streets at night, carrying a huge circular tray on her head and hauling along behind her the main focus of her life: a growing and increasingly gangly youth called Aye Kyu, pronounced 'EQ' by the town's NGO workers. This confused me, and for some time I wondered why Pan's son went under what appeared to be a code rather than a name. He was a likeable young man who dragged his feet along after his mother night after night, and was not in the least brutalised or even borderline feral as might be expected, but attended what he called 'monk school', where he acquired a basic education and some training in the Dharma. He was an indispensable aid to his mother as he could speak some English and Thai, bargain for her, and provide a sympathetic focus for her commercial activities. Pan invaded our calm evenings like that song you just can't get out of your head. Wherever you ate, whatever bar or cafe you tried to hide in, she would track you down and appear suddenly out of the night with tray and son and a toothless smile, whenever possible attempting to browbeat or shame anyone into buying anything from the Wheel which sustained her Life: the large round tray full of whatever she had picked up at the market that morning. This usually comprised yellow-and-red packets of sunflower seeds, deliciously savoury nuts still in their deep brown shells, plastic bags full of sweet yellow melon chunks, or, best of all, deep-fried potato slices in stapled packets. The potatoes were delicious, savoury explosions, but the staples posed a danger as they were easily lost in the contents of the packet. Pan descended on the cafes and bars every night, flogging her wares, at a substantial markup, to those of us who were fair game. Trying to avoid her advances was impossible as we were often caught in a well-planned pincer movement between Pan and EQ. EQ would smile and one might return it and politely turn away, only to be faced with Pan in all her moonlit glory, proffering the tray displaying her deal of the day. It is hard to imagine the sense of vulnerability and responsibility that Pan must have carried with her on her nightly perambulations. Rumours circulated about her mental health. EQ fell ill and Pan's prices went up to pay his medical fees. But when I think of Pan, I think of her as a survivor. If the Four Horsemen of the Apocalypse had ridden into town, Pan would have flogged them a packet of overpriced nuts. Whatever the cycle of history threw up – dictatorship, democracy or natural disaster – Pan would emerge carrying her tray. It was a precarious and, it appeared to me, quietly heroic life, and EQ got his education. The last I heard of him, he was working for an NGO. As for Pan, well, one hopes her business has been floated on the Singapore stock market.

But we who tread life's wheel can find ourselves wandering into its darker recesses. When exploring these twilit areas, a little scepticism may be prudent. A cluster of buildings which we will call the Anatar Orphanage and Learning Centre lies on the road winding up the Moei Valley. It occupies a muddy site and is comprised of a few bamboo huts and brutalist breeze-block constructions, which at that time housed sixty to seventy migrant kids. There are 'improving' signs on the walls with passages from the Bible. The head teacher, Pastor Johnny,[10] a well-built man of middle years with a new baby, had given up trying to get resettled in the USA in order to continue his work here. Apparently, he had adopted the name Johnny after an American folk-rock singer. He now dedicated himself to supporting some of the near-destitute families on the Thai border, especially those living in the no man's land of the tidal islands in the middle of the Moei River. It was youngsters from these villages who pushed cigarettes, booze and porn to anyone strolling by the river, and begged and scavenged around the town. Pastor Johnny told me that Burmese soldiers had even burnt the houses of these families, which I assume were hastily reconstructed. It appeared that he was a determined and compassionate man. I was also told that he and his wife lived on the leftovers of school meals and had risked arrest by cutting bamboo out of season for materials to build the school. Apparently, Johnny would visit the Friendship Bridge on the Moei and collect the kids living under the bridge. He tried to convince parents that education was good for their children but, I was told, some parents thought that putting their kids on the streets to beg was a better option as they could make 100 baht a day. One day I called in at the school with a young volunteer called Clare. She had been my assistant a number of years previously, in another life in England. She loved her work in the migrant schools, and was much loved in return. Johnny, smartly turned out in a red school T-shirt and blue sarong, wanted to bring out the kids to sing to us, but we had to move on. He said his goodbyes and, accompanied by the sound

---

10   Not his real name.

of pupils chanting, disappeared back into the cool of the classrooms to continue his mission. I never saw him again, but remembered him as one of the many people I met who struggled selflessly in some forgotten place. Or so I thought.

Reading the *Bangkok Post* of 22 December 2013, a headline caught my eye. Damning and cryptic – 'A Trust Betrayed' – it warranted further investigation. Three young girls, all children of Burmese migrant workers, had come to a boarding school, having been promised a brighter future:

> *But it appears their optimism was misplaced; the girls claim they were subjected to sexual abuse by the headmaster responsible for their welfare. The headmaster accused of the crimes in Mae Sot has since gone into hiding – he claims to escape threats from armed groups – and amid the lack of official facts it has become difficult to distinguish truth from innuendo and rumour in this bustling border town.*

To my huge embarrassment and shock, the final dark truth was revealed:

> *In police documents seen by Spectrum, however, facts began to separate from fiction. Following a month-long investigation, Mae Sot police have now issued a warrant for the arrest of the founder and headmaster of the [Anatar Orphanage and Learning Centre], who Spectrum[11] has decided to identify only as [Johnny].[12]*

---

11   A section in the *Post*.
12   I have altered the names of the school and its head teacher.

The name hit me like a punch in the dark. So, there it was. Johnny was on the run, and apparently had fled to the mountains on the Burmese side of the border. There was a huge scandal in Mae Sot, and measures were being taken to regulate the hitherto unregulated migrant schools which were, according to the Thais, 'learning centres' without the status – and presumably checks – afforded to a recognised school. It's inevitable that in an unregulated system there will be abuses. But who was Johnny – Pastor Johnny, in fact – who had taken the name of a rock star and was now a fugitive, and how does one balance the good against the ill?

I cite these cases as I feel that to have omitted them would have been a disservice to these communities. The immigrant community, like the refugee community, contained many extraordinary people who took into their hands their own destiny and that of their people. To portray people merely as victims would be to ignore their capacity for self-determination but, at the same time, it would be misleading to marginalise the vulnerability of migrant children living in these precarious circumstances. Many such human dramas were played out over a number of years, mirroring in their nobility and baseness the nature of the greater forces of history which were beginning to set in motion the wheels of change. As the cycle gradually brought in the promise of democracy, fear, anger and delusion began to stir in those with most to lose, and their inevitable response would create a growing momentum leading to the coup of 2021. In times without hope, one may take some comfort in the knowledge that all is subject to the laws of cause and effect, and that the bright eyes staring from moonlit faces would wait in anticipation for another turning of the wheel.

Taking Stock

For Those Who Wish to Go Down This Path

Don't expect people to be grateful. They are in a difficult situation, but they have pride. You are not in this for gratitude.

Be generous and kind. All human beings appreciate these qualities. They also open your heart.

Be honest with yourself. You can take some human satisfaction and enjoyment in achievement.

You and your team don't have all the answers. Listen to the local people and gradually get to know them. Try to meet them 'on their terms' within their own culture and mindset so that you begin to see the world through their eyes. This requires an understanding of their past as well as their current situation. So, take an interest in them, their lives, their history and their culture. And try to learn the language – this can open up relationships and a different world. The more effort you put into this the more people will take you seriously and understand that you are not in this as a short term 'operative', passing through and leaving when the novelty has worn off or the contract is up, but someone who is genuinely engaged with the context, issues and above all, the people themselves. This is especially important if you are building an organisation. Even if circumstances determine that you really are only there for a short term, taking this approach deepens your own experience and opens your eyes to the infinite variety of the world.

The British have a long history of individuals immersing themselves in other cultures, getting to know the people, valuing their traditions and supporting their causes often against great odds. Take some pride from the best of this tradition.

And don't sing 'Kumbaya'.

Children of the dump / John Cleary

Katharine and Toby

Migrant workers scavenging on dump

New Light Migrant School

MEP Mobile Unit Mawlamyine area

Mae La Karen Refugee Camp Pop.40,000

Refugees from attack on Myawaddy

Refugees flee from fighting in Myawaddy

KIA Officer 'The Sword of Gideon'   *Dim Mai 62 year old KIA Veteran*

Arrival of KIA unit (Gideon's Men)

KIA recruit training Mai Ja Yang_ Ann Pearce

Captain Dum Daw Gram Seng KIA - Atletico Madrid supporter

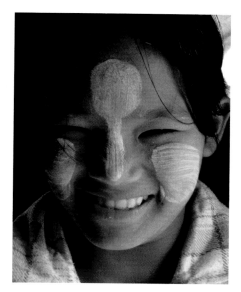

The Moon Face Matthew Gibbons

Wai Mar MEP Programme Director Burma

Pa Kahtawng IDP camp MJY _Ann Pearce

Playtime_ taken by migrant pupil

Fifteen

Burmese Haze[13] – Things are Not What they Appear to Be

A heat haze covered the Moei River. The white light shimmered over the surface of the water, blurring the boundaries between the real and the imagined. Certainty became vague and vagueness the norm. The haze flowed into and out of Burma's past, future, and especially its present, distorting reality, obscuring the truth and confusing its people.

Through my years working in Burma and along the Thai border, where life is precarious at the best of times, I found it useful to keep in mind what one of my former lecturers identified as the central message of Shakespeare. What, then, was this core wisdom? According to my tutor, it was 'Things are never what they appear to be'. As an organisation we pretty much adopted this as a guiding principle. Working in these conditions, certainty is vague

---

13   With apologies to George Orwell for ripping off his title "Burmese Days".

and the full truth elusive. Everything is seen through a heat haze. Everything is subject to impermanence.

Out of the haze on the river, something began to take shape: a black smudge moving slowly over the water. The smudge grew legs like a large aquatic spider. Gradually, the shape revealed its secret and very human tragedy, as is often the case with the truth in Burma. Sitting on, or clinging to, the huge inflated inner tube of a tyre were about a dozen people. In the broadest sense, they were migrants entering Thailand illegally. Legal entrance was now barred and the ironically and deceptively named Friendship Bridge closed due to some political dispute, but this did not discourage those who sought a better life or, at least, an escape from poverty. And the certainty of border closure had melted into a miasma of vaguery as the Burmese and Thai police who patrolled the riverbanks allowed the exodus to continue. A no, man's, land settlement had appeared on a sandbank in the middle of the river where makeshift shelters had been constructed, home to the boys who hustled cigarettes, cheap booze and porn. On the Burmese side of the river, decaying houses tumbled down to the banks, one with 'Fuck U' daubed on its crumbling concrete. It served as a greeting to anyone entering the country, a farewell to those leaving, and the junta's response to international criticism. It was depressing.

But the haze took on a life of its own and travelled much further than the Moei. In its efforts to confuse it had great ambitions and a much more extensive project in mind. The project was somewhat Orwellian in nature but it would be wrong to consider it a simple cynical manipulation of reality. The junta was not averse to lying, but it was convinced, or at least could present a case, that its versions of the truth were in the interests of 'the people'. It is difficult to say how far true conviction ever penetrated, but conformity to the mindset was required from all to some degree to ensure the success of The Project. To many this almost took the form of Orwellian doublethink, an acceptance of what it was necessary to believe in order to ensure one's physical survival and mental comfort.

So what, then, was The Project? First one must put all of this into a historical context. Nothing happens independently. Everything grows out of a process of cause and effect, which I will try to explain in the case of Burma. Following independence in 1948, the country had fallen into a decade of civil war and banditry waged by ethnic groups, communists and whoever had the guns. The Burmese army was weak and it took time to build its strength and stabilise the nation. These circumstances, as in so many similar situations elsewhere, led eventually to a military takeover and fear of a return to turmoil. What vision of the future, that grew out of these circumstances, did the generals have in mind for their long-suffering people? One immediate concern was the economy, and General Ne Win, having taken power in 1962, established the Burmese Socialist Programme Party (BSPP) and, in this one-party state, nationalised virtually everything. According to Ne Win's biographer, Robert Taylor, this was because Ne Win believed that the country needed economic as well as political independence and did not want to become reliant on either power bloc during the Cold War. The result was a disaster, leading in 1987 to Burma being named by the UN as one of the world's least developed countries. Further to this, the ruling military felt that the country required a gradual move towards a 'disciplined democracy'. But what was disciplined democracy? In his book *Buddhism, Politics and Political Thought in Myanmar* Matthew J. Walton addresses this issue. To understand the military's mindset we need to look at the beliefs of Theravada Buddhism, which for centuries have moulded Burmese thought. These hold that Man, by his very nature, is flawed and that without the mediating influences of Buddhism the *Pu Htu Zin* (the ordinary people) are motivated by the *kilethas* (defilements) of greed, envy, hatred, fear and delusion – in other words, the primal forces underlying self-interest. For democracy to succeed, as per The Project, correct moral practice was required, and this was not safe in the hands of the deluded masses. Who, then, would provide the guiding hand to lead onwards and upwards? The apparently undeluded military had the answer. They would take on the role of moral guardian and guide in order to ensure the construction of their disciplined democracy.

In her excellent book *Making Enemies*,[14] Mary Callahan suggests that the military had two key aims: to pacify the population, and to 'mould the Burmese people into a disciplined, dependable citizenry of a modern nation state'. She points to some early indications of Tatmadaw attitudes dating from as far back as 1958 when the Psywar Directorate (which was what its title suggests) circulated a paper headed *Some Reflections on Our Constitution*. This offers some fascinating revelations. According to Callahan it shows a 'profound distrust of the population [and] democracy'.[15]

---

14 *Making Enemies: War and State Building in Burma* by Mary P. Callahan (2004), p. 222.

15 Ibid. p.189

The distrust goes further to include the constitution itself, which guarantees freedom of speech and association. Without getting bogged down in the complexities of such documents, I can say that over the next half-century, right up to the present day, it is the constitution that is the bone of contention as it structures the future of the nation. As George Orwell might have put it, 'Who controls the present controls the constitution: who controls the constitution controls the future'. We shall return to this later as it provides the flashpoint for the chaos that was to consume the country in 2021.

It is on the subject of the Burmese people that the paper really begins to warm to its theme and give some idea of the shaping of the military mentality. It sees the people as 'apathetic' and open to manipulation by rebel groups using 'skilful propaganda'. Democracy is flawed because of the character of the masses, which is inclined towards 'egoism, personal interest and continuation of existence of survival at any costs whatsoever'. Given the circumstances that prevailed in Burma at the time I would have been inclined in the same direction. Comfortable longevity is a seductive goal! What this seems to imply is that the army saw itself as the defender of the people, but not in the conventional sense of combating some external foe. In fact, the people needed to be protected from themselves.

This stood somewhat in opposition to a more liberal, rights-based democracy favoured by Aung San Suu Kyi, also a devout Buddhist, and her vision of democracy is deeply informed by Buddhist principles. In her book, 'Freedom from Fear,' she acknowledges the key role that 'free men' must play in building 'a nation in which strong democratic institutions are firmly established as a guarantee against state-induced power...' but qualifies it with the assertion that those who wish to go down that rode, 'must first liberate their own minds from apathy and fear'.[16]

Here we have an acknowledgement of the negative forces that can afflict humanity. Further, Aung San Suu Kyi almost returns to the concept of the Dharma Razar (Divine King) of precolonial days; the benign ruler who follows the Dharma, the Buddhist path, in the interests of the people:

> *Rulers must observe the teachings of the Buddha.*
> *Central to these teachings are the concepts of truth,*
> *righteousness and loving kindness.*[17]

This part of the path seems to have escaped the military. So, in a way Aung San Suu Kyi sees personal liberation from 'defilements' as part of a national struggle for political liberation and moral governance. This is clear criticism of the military's version of a disciplined democracy which, at its worst, is something imposed on the people but somehow not on the military itself. All in all, the military had seemingly taken a rather selective view of Buddhism, and its promotion of disciplined democracy was nothing more than the creation of a system that would work in its own interest. This is where self-delusion, greed and fear –

16   As quoted in News Chant USA, 28th March 2021.
17   As quoted in *Buddhism, Politics and Political Thought in Myanmar* by Matthew J. Walton (2016), p. 184.

the defilements they attributed selectively to the ordinary people – infect the military itself. These guardians of the faith, the disciplined democrats, have become so caught up in the network of business and economic interests that keep them in the style to which they have become accustomed that they themselves have become – or perhaps have always been – motivated by the same defilements which form their criticism of the *Pu Htu Zin*. It needs a strong dose of delusion-packed doublethink to square their brutal actions with any high-flown moral crusade. But therein lies the fate of humanity. We package our baser instincts in a covering, a haze of moral piety, only to find, when we are fully aware and mindful, that our self-professed altruism works in harness with a motivating, and often destructive, self-interest. As William Golding described humanity in his profound work *Lord of the Flies*, we are a creature 'at once heroic and sick'. But that's the way we are. It's when we lose awareness of this and become deluded by our own propaganda that the trouble starts. So, as their people became refugees and migrants and fled the country, the generals continued to fuel their rather perverse vision of themselves as the Dharma Razar whose right to rule depends on their defence of the interests of the people. Any insurrection or dissension from an ethnic group or even groups within the Burman people themselves would be put down with sheer, unbridled brutality. Paradoxically, through the haze, the junta saw its own people as its enemies – or, at least, enemies of its national project.

Although Mary Callahan's research is taken from archival sources it's not difficult to see that these attitudes and values are deeply embedded in the military DNA.

In interviews with defecting officers in 2021 one can see their continuation and fruition.[18] The officers describe the Tatmadaw as a state within a state in which troopers are fed a particular ideology – with all its prejudices and delusions – that thicken the haze, as they work, socialise and marry within that bubble. Anyone who opposes the military is seen as a criminal, and democracy in the Western sense is an alien concept. Crucial to the understanding of the military psyche, they see themselves as guardians of a tradition and a faith that will crumble without them. They are led to believe that the nation is under a terminal threat from ethnic groups, Muslims and Western takeovers. Young soldiers caught in the haze feel that they are involved in a huge enterprise, the goal of which is nothing less than saving the nation. This, coupled with a profound fear of the consequences of disobedience, is a strong motivator. For the ordinary members of the 'poor bloody infantry' looking for something to believe in, this had a profound effect. Seeing themselves as guardians of the union in their minds legitimised their brutal actions. They were defenders of the faith as written by the generals, the latest incarnation of the Dharma Razar. And faith here is a key concept. This would have major significance in the cataclysmic events which would engulf Burma in 2021.

But the haze was not confined to the military. Under five decades of junta rule the media climate was one of the most restrictive on earth as the newspapers had to follow the government line. Ethnic groups were 'the enemy' bent

18 *Buddhism, Politics and Political Thought in Myanmar* by Matthew J. Walton (2016), p. 185.

on destroying the union, and the Rohingya were a threat to national culture. This was the diet fed to the *Pu Htu Zin*, playing on the *kilethas* of hatred, fear and delusion. After 2011 the print press's climate became a little more liberal but by that time the population had moved on to social media. In response, psyops took to Facebook, creating a source of much haze called the *Tatmadaw True News*. It was eventually rumbled by FB and banned for 'incitement of violence and coordinating harm'. So much for 'truth, righteousness and loving kindness'. Ethnic armed groups could also play this game. They, of course, had their own particular version of history, often focusing on their bitter experience at the hands of the Burmans. In many ways their nationalism mirrored that of the military, and their version of history did not lend itself to reconciliation. The haze was everywhere. And history, as Orwell knew, was the key:

> *Who controls the past controls the future: who controls the present controls the past.*
> (*Nineteen Eighty-Four* by George Orwell)

At this point a summary is needed, along with a firm reminder that none of this happened in a historical vacuum and history is complex and nuanced. The current situation is the result of cause and effect over many years. Two hundred years ago, aggressive Burman expansionism triggered the initial British invasion and humiliating defeat for the Burman Konbaung dynasty. In response to the impact of the West, the Konbaung made attempts to modernise the country. These changes led to political and economic instability which threatened British strategic and economic interests in the region and, after a third war, in 1885, the British eventually annexed the country, and took the drastic step of removing the king and dismantling the feudal fabric of Burman society.[19] There followed a process of economic, social and political modernisation within the limits of a colonial context but new ideas began to form of how an independent Burma might take shape in the modern world. However, competing interests, often ethnically based and predating the annexation by the British, were present and were, arguably, deepened by colonial rule. For example, the British initially barred the Burmans from being part of the armed forces and favoured the 'hill tribes', thereby increasing Burman resentment. A world war pitted one set of loyalties against another. Out of colonial rule and international conflict grew an independent Burma with a fledgling democracy. Independence failed to meet the aspirations of ethnic groups, and this led to civil war. Government broke down and chaos ensued. At this point, enter the military, now under Burman command, with a mission to 'save the nation' (probably from itself), and eventually to serve its own interests. The generals also reflected on history! Cause and effect, action and reaction – Burma's karmic wheel continues to spin.

I have written this not as an apologist for the actions of the Burmese military, but to try to understand, and perhaps provide something of an explanation of, how and why this can happen. It is dangerous to think that these things are done by monsters. They are done by human beings, and

---

19   See Thant Myint-U, *The Making of Modern Burma*, Chapter 8

we must understand the conditions that make us act in this way. The haze can affect us all. Fear, self-interest and a misguided sense of mission can influence our actions, leading to a loss of our sense of interconnectedness. Good people can do evil things if motivated by delusion, anger and fear which prevent them from seeing, through the haze, their humanity and that of others. Over time, the haze flowed through the barracks into the city suburbs, to the small towns and across the rice paddies to the isolated villages, rising to the hills and flowing down the great valley of the Irrawaddy. Reality blurred and reassembled itself into delusion. Neighbours became enemies; monks peddled hatred and fear; threats were all around, undermining the nation; uncertainty and insecurity prevailed. Nothing was quite what it seemed to be as the country wandered through its midsummer night's dream, leading gradually and inexorably towards a nightmare.

Moving On

2011–2014

The NLD, led by Aung San Suu Kyi, had refused to register for and contest the November 2010 elections. Their absence offered an open field to the military-backed parties, and a quasi-civilian government run by former generals had taken power. From then on there appeared to be just a ray of hope for the country's future. The new president, Thein Sein, himself a former general, seemed, in comparison to what had come before, reasonable, ready to talk to the West, and less orientated towards China. He wore a suit.

On 1 April 2012 by-elections were held for forty-five vacant seats. The NLD won forty-three of the forty-four it contested, predicting a landslide victory in the 2015 general election. The West began to warm to Burma and, of course, was ready to win it over from its allegiance to China. America's president, Barack Obama and the UK's prime minister, David Cameron both visited in 2012.

After years of working under the radar, BEP was now officially recognised by the local Thai education office. It was a moving day when, accompanied by Graham McNeil, an old friend and our company secretary, we signed a Memorandum of Understanding. The country began to open up and become more NGO-friendly. Hope had not dawned but there was a glimmer of light, a breath of air.

Be warned: stick to the central message of Shakespeare – 'things are not what they appear to be'.

Sixteen

Into Burma

Moses, Sheldrakes and a Scorpion, Mon State, Burma, March 2014

By the old Moulmein Pagoda, lookin' lazy at the sea,
There's a Burma girl a-settin', and I know she thinks o' me;
For the wind is in the palm-trees, and the temple-bells they say:
"Come you back, you British soldier; come you back to
Mandalay!"
(*Mandalay* by Rudyard Kipling)

For those of you not familiar with the geography of Burma, let me point out that Moulmein is nowhere near Mandalay. Four hundred miles and a ten-hour journey by road separate the two towns. Kipling was, of course, aware of this, but why let fact ruin romance?! Kipling's pagoda in Moulmein (or 'Mawlamyine' as it is pronounced – seductively with gentle, rather languid tones – in Burmese) is the Kyaikthanlan Pagoda, which has spectacular views overlooking the lovely town with its colonial architecture, neatly laid-out park, Victorian railway station, clock tower and, remarkably, an obelisk.

The junta, in one of its more chameleon-like phases, had swapped its uniforms for business suits and, following something resembling a general election in 2010 (without the participation of the main opposition, Aung San Suu Kyi's NLD) and then by-elections in 2012 (with the participation of the NLD, which won most of the seats) had established a quasi-civilian government run, unsurprisingly, by a former general. For MEP, who for years had been working in the refugee camps of the Thai border, opportunities inside Burma began to open up.

I had spent a day travelling from the border, where we had projects to deliver, to Moulmein and, after a night's rest, headed for the Kyaikthanlan Pagoda. A kind of Kiplingesque karma was in play here as I had just arrived at the main pagoda platform, made the obligatory merit-making donation and received a certificate of proof (always best to have the paperwork when dealing with reincarnation), when I was accosted for a photo by a rather ample young Burmese lady. It was an uncanny 'Kipling moment', with the breeze from the sea moving the palms, the tinkling of the bells, and a real-live Burmese girl. I was on the point of asking if she had been waiting long when my delusion was broken by the arrival of her mother, father, aunts, uncles, sisters and entourage of friends, all wanting to pose for pictures with a rare and exotic sight: not the array of temple statues resplendent in blues, reds and gold, but a rather pale and bewildered Englishman. I was now amongst the Mon.

So who, amongst Burma's seemingly inexhaustible supply of ethnic groups, are the Mon? They call themselves 'the people of the golden sheldrake'. As the image of a sheldrake may not spring readily to mind, I will explain. A sheldrake is a rather large duck, sometimes sporting a quite racy little head plumage. In our colder northern climes it can be brown and white, but in the land of myth its plumage is brilliantly golden, and in the Mon foundational myth the origins of the name and imagery are charming and filled with supernatural potency. The story goes something like this. In the distant past the Mon lands were submerged beneath the sea, but all that would change when the Buddha, on a 'flight' over Southeast Asia, encountered two sheldrakes (*hamsa* in Burmese), the female perched on the back of the male (there is significance in this pose, which I will come to later), occupying a rocky outcrop jutting from the sea. The Buddha prophesied that a great kingdom would emerge from the sea and its people would glorify Buddhism.[20] This is worth mentioning here as it bears relevance to the part MEP was later to play in education in Mon State.

And a great kingdom did indeed grow up in what is now southern Burma, with its capital Hongsawaddy, suitably founded by the deity Indra, situated on the spot where the sheldrakes had been sighted. The Mon kingdom flourished but, after a series of wars with the Burmans ending in the middle of the eighteenth century, was eventually destroyed. Notably, the 'hammer of the Mon' was the Burman King Alaungpaya, now the favourite of the military with a statue looming over the huge parade ground at the new capital, Naypyidaw.

---

20   *Mon Nationalism and Civil War in Burma: The Golden Sheldrake* by Ashley South, pp. 52–3.

Alaungpaya is credited with 'unifying' Burma. In practice this meant the subjugation of (amongst others) the Mon and the subsequent decline of their language and culture. Alaungpaya even renamed an ancient religious centre Rangoon, meaning 'end of strife' or, more chillingly for the Mon, 'annihilation of the enemy'. However, the Mon remembered their heroes of the resistance against the Burmans, and one in particular was renowned. This was the Smin Daw, who had fought against the Burmese in various incarnations over the years and had enjoyed success as a guerrilla fighter. They also kept alive the idea of the Min Laung, the future king, a kind of Arthurian figure who would reappear in a new incarnation and re-establish Mon sovereignty.

Inevitably, as with everything in Burma, the British got involved somewhere down the line and arrived in 1825, hence the period piece that is Moulmein. Although Mon nationalism revived at times, encouraged occasionally by the British, and there was even open warfare against the Burman state, the Mon never regained their independence. However, that aspiration never died. They kept their beloved *hamsa*, the golden sheldrake, which can be seen everywhere. The Burmese military government allowed the use of the sheldrake for Mon State, but theirs was different: standing inert and grounded. For the Mon, however, their bird continued to soar in golden splendour. It encapsulated the hope of the return of the Min Laung in some form, and there were many Smin Daws in the hills, ready to help. In the '70s the Mon launched an armed insurrection against the military dictatorship. Smin Daw was back, now armed with a Kalashnikov and flying a red flag featuring a rather streamlined golden duck. It was the same story, more or less, that we had encountered with the Karen and would face again and again inside Burma. Although a ceasefire of sorts had been arranged in 1995, there was still sporadic fighting and internal displacement. In 2020 ReliefWeb reported a Mon IDP's view of the situation:

> *"We have no land to return even though we desperately want to. We want to stay where we are right now and wish that the NMSP[21] is able to achieve a sustainable peace agreement. We want our children to be able to study well at school and our areas to be developed when there is a lasting peace."*

Her heartfelt statement echoed the aspirations of many thousands of people inside and outside the country displaced by decades of war. Instability had an effect on the labour force in Mon State and on our future role.

One thing was booming in Mon State and that was what the Mon called 'white gold': raw rubber. Families were moving out of the 'unstable' areas and taking work in the rubber plantations. They were internal migrants and their children needed education, and, after years learning our trade on the Thai border, this was where we came in. So, I undertook the journey to Mon State to look at the country's current condition and discuss possible projects. One potential partner was the Mon National Education Committee, with whom I had made contact. It was the first time I had been inside Burma for nearly twenty years.

The journey to Moulmein from Mae Sot had been

---

21 New Mon State Party.

a journey through the layers of Burmese history. Some friends had arranged for a driver to pick me up in the town of Myawaddy on the Burmese side of the border, where my real journey would begin. Arriving through the Burmese customs into Myawaddy's main street is rather overwhelming, with taxis touting for trade, would-be guides hustling their skills, street sellers trying to capture your attention, and the sun cooking you inch by baking inch. I was beckoned into a car by a young man in a red T-shirt and jeans, a young couple jumped into the back, and we were off. I could not pick up the language, but it was my first encounter with the language of the Mon, a musical, appropriately birdlike tongue very different from Burmese or Karen. Pushing out of Myawaddy, past the temple with the massive red-and-green concrete crocodile, we soon found ourselves in a quite arid landscape and pulled off the narrow tarmac road onto a dirt track. At times like these a kind of creeping, low-level panic starts to take hold as one begins to wonder if one is in the right place, with the right company, going in the right direction. We stopped at the foot of a small hill crowned by a bamboo-and-concrete bunker-like structure and waited. For what, I was uncertain, but suddenly coming down the hill towards us was a man in black shorts, a singlet and an army-issue camouflage hat. A fine assortment of tattoos covered his arms and legs and he carried a pistol in a shoulder holster marked 'Police'. Moments such as these can be, to say the least, unsettling, and this one spiralled quickly into the bizarre when the man in black descended from the hill, pushed his head into the car, smiled through his beard and announced, with almost biblical authority, "I am Moses."

My hesitant reply of "Pleased to meet you" somehow didn't quite meet the occasion.

So who, then, was this Moses? The driver signalled that he would return, and the car pulled away, leaving the young couple and me in the company of our armed companion, who pointed to the bunker at the top of the hill. We offered no resistance. It was rather like being taken hostage, in a benign kind of way. The bunker, which was still under construction, brought further surprises. A concrete wall supported a rather precarious half-completed timber roof with some beams in place and others yet to find a secure lodging. But it was what was hanging from the beams that grabbed my attention. Rather than tablets of stone, Moses was in possession of a small armoury. Automatic weapons and pistols hung from nails, but pride of place went to a World War II carbine. He could probably have defended the hill against a battalion of Burmese, but this was not the building's function. "This is the Karen Youth Organisation," Moses announced in good English. Given the decor I wouldn't have guessed that it was a branch of the local YMCA. Moses could see that I was interested, and that got him onto his pet topic: the current ceasefire with the Burmese army and the need for young Karen to know about their history. History, identity, tradition; these are themes one encounters again and again in this country riven by civil strife.

I warmed to Moses; he was a man of some presence and charisma and seemed very committed to his work. The hill was a rather pleasant spot, catching the cool breezes blowing down the valley and providing a panoramic vista of the hills that rolled out to the north. It was almost a romantic scene, with the white stupas rising from the higher peaks standing out against an azure sky. In Buddhist thought, one of the functions of a stupa is to harmonise the environment in which it is built and subdue the chaotic forces at work there. However, this was Karen State, the scene of a war that had been going on for half a century. This was the route the Japanese army had taken when they had invaded Burma in late 1941. I reflected on the history of the carbine so prized by my new friend. However, unlike the Israelites, the Karen had found their promised land, and this was it. Deserts they now had to cross and seas that would need to be parted stood as metaphors for the struggles that still lay ahead, but I was certain that Moses would lead his people in the right direction. I hoped the stupas would help.

In a cloud of dust, our driver and car reappeared at the foot of the hill, but instead of T-shirt and jeans the driver now wore full KNLA uniform. This would make sense as the journey progressed. Two hours and about five miles later we were stuck in an endless queue of traffic crossing the Dawna Range on the only road into Burma. It was noticeable that the traffic was only going one way, and that was from Thailand into Burma. The reason for this was that it was Wednesday. The road is the old Japanese military road, cut through the mountains in 1941. It is not much wider than a large truck or mule train, and given its original purpose, that would make sense. On one side the sheer grey cliff face rises from the roadside, and on the other there is a merciless drop into the jungle below. Serving as grim warnings to anyone tempted to take a chance, wheels, exhausts and the undercarriages of unlucky vehicles poke out from the rocks and bushes on the drop side. No one attempted to overtake today. The Japanese were single-minded in their attempts to take Burma from the British. They invaded via this road with high hopes, and one wonders about their condition as they slogged back along it three years later. But on Wednesdays the traffic went from east to west. On Thursday it would flow in the opposite direction. Getting the wrong day would be disastrous if you were in the transport business, and transport was the business on the old military road. Trucks were piled high with every sort of commodity. We were in a kind of convoy that looked like a small, moving range of hills. Sacks of rice, boxes of canned food, and baskets of vegetables formed peaks on the back of lorry after lorry, and on top of them, like successful mountaineers, sat groups of men and women wearing every known kind of headgear from hoods to conical bamboo hats. The convoy inched forward, gears and brakes grinding on the steep gradient, each truck spewing out clouds of black exhaust.

We reached the top of the ridge and then began the winding descent to the flat Burmese plain that stretched out into the hazy distance towards the Gulf of Martaban. We were moving deeper into Burma, and what began to appear on either side of the road as we reached the plain was not rice paddies but something with a more industrial feel. Scattered for thirty yards into the fields, plastic bags, bottles, cups and containers covered the greenery like a multicoloured fungus. We pulled into a spacious, open roadside cafe with forty to fifty large tables and a corrugated WC that was far too dangerous to use. Most men didn't. I found a bench opposite a burly tattooed man wearing an AC/DC shirt and, wary of the local fare, munched self-consciously through a packet of crisps. People ate quickly under the gaze of large posters of an implacable Aung San Suu Kyi and her uniformed father. A politically themed 'motorway cafe' said something about the country. The noise was constant, with waitresses shouting out orders to the kitchen, the cooks shouting back and the diners calling to the waitresses who, carrying plates piled with noodles, vegetables and fried chicken, navigated the tables with an almost gymnastic nimbleness and martial dedication to duty. The smell of wet earth mingled with that of frying garlic as boys wielding red-and-yellow plastic jerrycans hurled water over the overheated wheels and brakes of lorries, creating clouds of hissing steam which floated over the diners. A low-intensity cockfight was taking place on the other side of the road, but in the baking heat neither bird showed much interest. A few mangy dogs lurked in the shade. This was my first taste of Burma in nearly twenty years. Aung San Suu Kyi was no longer under house arrest and was openly the poster girl for a nation on the move.

We were soon back on the road and an interesting problem began to emerge. The traffic kept to the right-hand side. This seemingly normal regulation hides an odd story and requires some explanation. The British left Burma in 1948 and for the next twenty-two years everyone continued to drive, in good British style, on the left. However, on 6 December 1970, General Ne Win decreed that from now on the country would switch to the right. This was a sudden and radical change, and the reasons for it remain unclear. There is some suggestion that Ne Win had noticed on his travels that most countries drove on the right, and felt that Burma would have to link up with international road networks. However, nothing so prosaic would be allowed to get in the way of much creative speculation. Ne Win was, according to many accounts, a superstitious man and, as recounted earlier, allegedly changed the 50-kyat note to 45 as the latter's two digits totalled nine, his lucky number. A similar theory holds that his wife's astrologer told him that it would be better for the country if people started driving on the right. His critics claim that he misinterpreted the astrologer's advice, which was, in fact, that he should shift the economic model to capitalism rather than the leftist socialist road he was taking and which did indeed lead to economic meltdown. Driving on the right was clearly ill advised, as ninety per cent of the cars imported into the country had right-hand drives! Overtaking anything on these narrow, badly surfaced roads was now marginally suicidal.

Our uniformed driver, however, was not to be intimidated. Holding tightly behind one of the mountainous juggernauts, a decision had to be made: overtake on the left-hand side even though you couldn't see the oncoming traffic, or veer off the road into the fields and take the lorry from the inside? Both were attempted during our teeth-clenching ride. Sympathetic lorry drivers sometimes took pity on the motorist and flashed their right-hand rear indicators to signal that the road ahead was clear and it was safe to overtake. This required a strong nerve, a level of blind faith, and a sympathetic insurance company. However, one other obstacle to our safe passage began to emerge. Every few miles the traffic slowed as it approached a sandbagged guard post and a red-and-white barrier across the road. These 'toll gates' are found all over Burma and provide income for whoever is in charge of the road. This is a really easy source of income for the myriad of armed groups that exist in the country. Some toll gates are manned by the regular army and others by various ethnic armed organisations (EAOs). The soldiers manning the first gates were Karen, and this explained why our driver had changed into uniform. We breezed, toll free, through the gates controlled by the smartly turned-out young men of the KNLA, and even managed to slip through those manned in a more relaxed way by the Burmese army controlling the bridges. The ceasefire may have accounted for the latter's easy manner and smiles.

Grateful for our survival, we too were almost deliriously happy as we drove into Moulmein, which for me meant a cool room at the pink-and-yellow curiously named Cinderella Hotel. Maybe, I speculated, it stood as a rags-to-riches metaphor for a country coming out of years of stagnation under a military dictatorship. You can suffer from delusion after surviving the road to hell on a packet of crisps. At ground level Moulmein, rather than a Cinderella, is something of a Miss Havisham of a town: once loved, then neglected and now frozen in time. The British were here from 1827 onwards and their mark is everywhere. A grid of streets leads down to the Strand esplanade along the waterfront. The old colonial buildings are rather shabby and in need of a coat of paint and some serious plastering. Buildings which should have been listed and maintained have been left to rot. The pavements are cracked, and once-grassy areas have become dust bowls and are often the territory of semi-feral dogs. The red-and-white clock tower, bearing the grand inscription, 'This Clock Tower was erected to the memory of the King Emperor Edward

VII by the citizens of Moulmein', is a prominent focal point. The clock was working, and its chimes rang across the park as they had since 1912. George Orwell would have heard those same chimes during his time in the imperial police force in Moulmein. His mother had grown up in the town and would have enjoyed the park. However, the park was completely empty every time I passed. The junta's economic disaster of the 1980s, brought on mainly by its peculiar brand of state socialism, had also left its mark with a Soviet-style monument on the central roundabout. Workers in blue overalls and carrying hammers stood shoulder to shoulder with an array of armed men. It would have looked charming in North Korea. I wondered if the Burmese actually used towns in the same way as the British, and had a strange sense that some districts seemed 'occupied' rather than lived in. The whole setting of Moulmein is a delight, with golden pagodas glinting on the headlands of the bay which embrace a town waiting, like Miss Havisham, for someone to love her. I hoped that whoever that would be would respect her unique charm and personality. The rush to 'modernity' is seductive and its concrete blandness a curse which invariably turns 'somewhere' into 'anywhere'.

Moulmein University is vast. Its classical portico is grand and its entrance hall cool, dark and cavernous. It was also empty. The students were just being allowed back after years of sporadic education and suspension due to government paranoia. The government saw the universities as hotbeds of sedition, but the only potential for insurrection at the moment seemed to come from a flock of birds who had stubbornly made the vast foyer their home. Meeting an old friend who now ran an NGO based at the university provided a window on the Mon world. He explained that the problem was the military. The army was a state within a state with fingers in many rather tasty pies. Becoming part of 'the system' is an attractive proposition for many young men, especially those who are well connected. I was never certain how the profits from any 'graft' actually filtered down to the 'poor bloody infantry'. Perhaps better not to ask. The situation in Mon State was dire. Education was not equipping the young people for a changing economic and social system. Jobs were being taken by better-educated young people from Yangon, brought in by companies setting up in the area. The biggest form of employment was unskilled labour in the rubber plantations that churned out the 'white gold'. But my friend loved the town, the relative peace, the fine-looking Mon people, the temples, the sea; taken together, they created a visual and spiritual beauty. I could see his point.

The following day, spiritual matters were not a priority at the office of the Mon National Education Committee (MNEC). Identity and cultural survival were at the heart of so much of what was happening in Burma. Many Mon saw the increasing dominance of education, and just about everything else, by the culture of the Burman majority as a threat to Mon culture and language. With cultural preservation in mind, in 1992 the New Mon State Party had set up 'Mon national schools' and 'Mon language schools', mainly in Mon State. In 1995 the Smin Daws of the armed wing of the Mon resistance hung up their guns and signed a ceasefire. From then on the number of Mon schools began to increase and they came under the direction of the MNEC. The Mon system delivered basic education up to Grade 9, and from then on pupils fed into the wider state system. I sensed that this was an uneasy alliance. The MNEC is run by petite Mon ladies with such ferocious determination that you draw the conclusion that their main source of energy must be raw meat. They are a formidable bunch led by two former refugees: the redoubtable Mi Yin, a small, lively lady of middle years, supported by the deceptively delicate, bespectacled figure of Mi Lay[22]. Damning the Burmese government and NGO funding policy with dignified bitterness, they had a plan for teacher training and English language development. They knew what they wanted and were still smarting after previous requests for funding had been turned down. Like Miss Havisham, they would not take rejection lightly, I guessed, and I pondered my own fate should I fail. "Yes, English is needed," they explained, "but we don't want Mon State to be like India." I wasn't sure exactly what that meant – maybe Kipling was to blame. Despite the warning against linguistic colonisation (and having probably consumed a pound of the local version of steak tartare earlier in the day), over the next two hours these charming but determined ladies detailed a programme that would require a sizeable bid to the Big Lottery Fund UK (which it later did). There is no word for 'compromise' in Burmese, and in the birdlike language of the Mon I suspect the basic concept is dangerously vague. The following day I returned for a second battering. This time we met at the Mon Women's Association. Men were definitely surplus to requirements, and an etching of Miss Havisham above the door would have set the scene. Two more grinding hours

---

22   Not real names

on the master plan and Big Lottery bid accompanied by much tearful criticism of the failure of foreign funding bodies to support the MNEC. These slight, graceful ladies – speaking, in keeping with their national symbol, birdlike Mon – were daughters of the sheldrake, but their duck was built to industrial standards. Meat (notably lightly boiled, probably as a concession to me) was served by a team of rather stern interns, and then I was allowed to leave. Riding pillion on a motorbike taxi, I was oblivious to the charms of Moulmein. I now realised the prophetic symbolism of the two sheldrakes in the Mon creation fable. The female was seated on the male. They knew the score.

That night I sat in the corner of the Thanlwin Restaurant, hoping to reflect on the day. My hope was in vain. This was a noisy, bustling place with a heavily built major-domo in a green Mon *longyi* directing the young waiters in flip-flops and T-shirts who scurried from table to table. It all seemed to run like clockwork: tables were cleared, guests seated and meals served. However, that was a minor miracle as the major-domo was, remarkably, mute. The only sound the poor chap could make was an ear-piercing scream as if some ghostly apparition had suddenly appeared to disrupt the proceedings. However, this, followed by a dramatic hand signal, was sufficient to terrify the waiters and send them hurtling at full speed to complete their assigned tasks. It was amazing to watch; a tour de force. The place was packed. A family group of fifteen to twenty people with grey-haired grandfather at the head of the table laughed and argued over incoming plates of vegetables, meat and noodles. The major-domo screamed and pointed at seemingly multiplying apparitions, the terrified waiters scuttled from table to table and an American action movie, ignored by everyone, blasted from the TV sets hanging from the ceiling and provided the soundtrack to the proceedings. A perfect evening.

The following day I faced the return journey. This time, riding shotgun (M16 under the seat, I was told), was a major from a special branch of the KNLA to ensure our safe passage through the checkpoints. The other passengers were two young ladies, a middle-aged man chewing betel, and a monk with interesting tattoos. The monk took the front seat (you quickly get to know your place in the Burmese pecking order), and, accompanied by 'Sutter's Mill' on the sound system, in high spirits we drove out of Moulmein on our shared adventure. The sun was coming up and a hazy light hung over the fields. We drifted over the huge suspension bridge spanning the misty Thanlwin River and through the checkpoints without a hitch; the major had taken special care to attach a KNLA sticker to the windscreen. 'American Pie' and, appropriately, 'Country Roads' accompanied us through the low-lying rice paddies, and as we approached the mountains the company mellowed with 'Wonderful Tonight' and a selection of Mark Knopfler hits. The young ladies had been travel-sick from the outset and marked our passage with a trail of plastic bags dropped delicately from the window. Emerging suddenly from a set of buildings to our right, a group of youths in fatigues and carrying automatic weapons ran in a line along the side of the road. This was the Burmese army out on exercises. The officer pulled them into some kind of order as we passed; a file of skinny boys in flip-flops and wearing uniforms several sizes too big. The moment seemed most bizarre as we passed displaying the sign of the rebels, the KNLA, and bashing out the best of Dire Straits. It's the small kindnesses you remember: the gentleman with the wad of betel in his cheek buying me a can of Elephant beer and carefully wiping the top with a tissue; the monk offering me a cool towelette at a wayside stop; the attempts by all to make some conversation in broken English.

As we drove out of the mountains towards the Thai border I tried to gather my impressions of Burma after a twenty-year gap. The more you knew, the more complex the future looked: a country seemingly awakening after years of neglect, the tragedy of internal displacement, the delightful and determined Mon ladies building a better future, the lack of opportunity and a flawed education system, not to mention the spectre of civil strife and violence still brooding in the hills and forests and lurking at the roadblocks. The monk slung his bare arm over the back of the seat as we cruised towards the border post. There, as if almost alive, tattooed into his forearm was a scorpion with sting raised. In the non-dualistic Buddhist world, the scorpion is the symbol of transformation. No one and nothing is permanently evil. Everyone contains the *boddicitta*, the Buddha heart capable of compassion and wisdom, and if the scorpion can be transformed then so can we all. It was a hopeful sign for a country which needed hope in these years of its own transformation.

Seventeen

Gap Weekends

Leadership, Visions and a Better World, Thai-Burmese Border

It's the waste of life that gets to you even after years of this kind of work, and especially the waste of young lives. It's genuinely heartbreaking to see young people confined to refugee camps for years; bright kids who should have a future, just wasting away behind barbed wire. Any human being with a modicum of compassion would want to do something. Youngsters in the West go for 'gap years'. Their counterparts in refugee camps on the Thai border can't even get a gap weekend... or, as we shall see, perhaps they could?

The idea came after our association with the wonderful Harrow International School, Bangkok, had developed over a couple of years. The Karen stuck in camps on the Thai border were totally realistic about their plight. They were in this for the long haul. No one was going home soon, but some were up for resettlement in the West. You may remember that the largest camp, Mae La, contained a model Western kitchen for those about to be resettled to ponder, and for the rest of the camp to wonder at its shiny magnificence. But the resettlement programme was coming to a close. Those left in the camps would have to sit it out on the border and miss out on the kitchen experience. Many had one eye on eventually going home, or what was left of home after land grabs had eaten into their rice paddies, their villages had been burnt and their fields littered with landmines. I personally would have gone for the new kitchen, but that wasn't how some of the Karen saw it. Many had given their lives to the dream of a semi (or fully) autonomous state, Kawthoolei, often translated as 'Land of Flowers'. Dreams! Something to believe in! Something to make life worth living and give it purpose. This was for their children, for the future, for a new generation, but many were now grinding out their lives in refugee camps. A new country needs leaders, an educated class, young people proud of their heritage and ready to build a future. Unfortunately, some of the Karen's best and brightest were languishing in the camps, being tempted by resettlement to the land of white goods.

So, what were the Karen to do? They came up with a plan. They would set up a network of specialist colleges to provide further education. Now, this may be fine if you are somewhere comfortable and stable with lots of resources, human and material, but the Thai–Burmese border was not Sweden. Nevertheless, they did it. A string of specialist colleges, funded by foreign donors, was set up across several of the camps. One specialised in education, another health, and others in community and business management.

Students would decide on their area of specialism and go and live as boarders in the camp where the college teaching their particular choice was located. The courses could last for up to four years, so this was a long-term commitment. The first two years were given over to general/foundation subjects and the last two to the specialist area. One of their problems was that any qualification coming out of a college in a refugee camp had limited standing. This was where we came in.

We received an invitation to deliver a Cambridge English course, complete with exams and international certification, at the grandly named Pu Taw Memorial Junior College (PTMJC) in Mae La camp. PTMJC specialised in education and the last two years of the course were delivered mainly in English. We couldn't resist the offer and, with some funding from a kind donor, set up the six-month course. Harrow, Bangkok, offered to provide examiners and, with great munificence, pay candidates' entry fees. David Eastgate and Dava Romyanond, who had done such sterling work in the migrant schools, would lead the team of examiners. It's interesting at this point to draw comparisons between the two seemingly different schools. Harrow's original school in England had educated twenty-three Thai Princes, so it seemed natural that its first Asian branch should be established in Bangkok. Harrow's campus was vast, high-tech and catered for, in general, boys and girls who may become leaders in their chosen fields. PTMJC comprised two or three concrete, corrugated iron and bamboo structures on a hill in the middle of Mae La camp, then home to forty thousand refugees. Its material resources were limited and its library contained shelves of dusty and, most likely, unread and unreadable books provided by well-meaning but ill-advised donors. I remember seeing one such library displaying, side by side, copies of *The Easter Bunny That Ate My Sister* and *Lessons for Soviet Youth*. The visions of Western culture these conjured up are beyond belief. In addition, in PTMJC high-tech equipment was conspicuously absent. In spite of this, the two establishments were not exactly a million miles apart. Harrow, Bangkok, had adopted the motto 'Leadership for a Better World', and its ethos was imbued with that sense of community activism, involvement, and the development of leadership qualities. It was led by a dynamic head, Mick Farley, strongly supported by his second master Tim Jefferis, and an equally dynamic master in charge of the Leadership in Action element of the Harrow programme, Brian van den Berg. PTMJC, though in many ways relatively modest, had equivalent aspirations for its young people.

Actually getting to PTMJC was something akin to embarking on a medieval pilgrimage. Mae La camp was vast and there were several entry points in the barbed-wire perimeter. These were usually simple bamboo gates manned by a Thai soldier sitting under a pandanus-leaf shelter. He didn't have a lot to do. Intrusions into his day were generally limited and something of an occasion. His walkie-talkie crackled irritatingly from time to time. He had a book; not a novel but a huge ledger in which you wrote your name and other details, invariably with a pink biro; obviously army issue. Passport and camp pass checked, a push on the creaking gate brought you into another world. This was Mae La camp, the vast bamboo town which stretched for almost two miles. The path fell away steeply from the gate towards a stream. Descent was tricky. The gravel-and-clay surface was loose, and losing footing always resulted in scrapes full of grit and oozing blood. A bamboo bridge traversed a fast-flowing stream, the home of red-faced Muscovy ducks. Litter washed down from the market further upstream swirled in the waters. Camp dogs, hot and bad-tempered, sniffed around. A greasy earth-and-concrete path climbed almost vertically from the stream. Without crampons, it could only be negotiated by walking side-foot first. Steps were cut into difficult sections, but they were often run through with ankle-spraining tree roots. One eventually arrived at a small, dusty plateau and was faced, unexpectedly, by nothing less than a golden bust on a golden plinth, glittering in the tropical sun like an idol from a lost civilisation. This was no idol nor medieval saint, but the image of a senior Karen man sporting the most magnificent moustache and looking 'the very model of a modern major general', as Messrs Gilbert and Sullivan would have it. Baden-Powell would have snapped to attention in his presence. This was Pu Taw. A much-venerated leader of the Karen, he now stood as a symbol of paternalism and leadership. Under his stern but kindly countenance was a large golden plaque inscribed, in English:

A vision without a task is a mere dream.
A task without a vision is drudgery.
A vision with a task is the hope of the world.

It could have graced a sonnet! In fact it may have done, as here the English–Karen link reveals itself again, as these words reputedly appear on a church wall in Sussex and date back to about 1730. This was clearly meant to inspire 'Leadership for a Better World', the Harrovian principle contained in its motto of a vision linked to action. Bamboo and barbed wire do not confine human aspiration. Behind the statue stood the rather less imposing concrete-and-corrugated-iron buildings of the school and its office. The school dog, a Labrador called Mr Black, lay on the steps, panting in the heat. As English public schools have their portraits of national figures and former headmasters, on entering the PTMJC office one was surrounded by portraits of senior Karen, suitably moustached. However, in total contrast to the rather hirsute leaders of old was the current college principal, Khu Paw, a relatively young, very elegant and extremely competent Karen lady. She had been educated in India and spoke fluent English. She came from a senior Karen family and, having missed opportunities for resettlement due to studying in India at that time, the college was her life. I never did ask her what she thought about the model kitchen. It might have been a delicate subject.

So, to return to the key issue, what of the 'gap weekend'? In effect, it was the answer to a problem we had encountered. We could provide a Cambridge English course and Harrow examiners would deliver the exams. There would be difficulties. We had to go through the Thai authorities to get a teacher into the camp, and we would have to take thirty to forty young students out of the camp to Mae Sot for the exams. This would involve much paperwork from us and general goodwill from the Thai camp captain, but it could be done. In March 2013 we duly organised the first exams for a contingent of students from PTMJC. It was a high-pressure couple of days for everyone, but it was successful. However, David, Dava and other examiners from Harrow noted one particular difficulty. The Karen had not performed too well in the spoken part of the exam. The reason for this was not difficult to ascertain. Questions in this section were almost standardised. Candidates were asked to talk about the activities in their lives, places they had visited and, possibly the most culturally agonising question for the Karen, 'What do you do during your holidays?' This was all fine for someone who lived what may be called a 'normal' existence, but in a refugee camp, life was limited and routine and lacked variety. They had almost nothing to talk about. This had to be addressed, but under the circumstances, how could this possibly be done? The answer was a 'gap weekend'.

Brian van den Berg at Harrow came up with the simple and quite brilliant idea of including this educational project as part of their Leadership in Action programme. They would bring a group of Harrow youngsters, about the same age as the Karen students, to Mae Sot, and we would pull strings to get the Karen students out of the camp for a weekend. It would be called, grandly, a 'cultural exchange', and include a variety of shared activities. This was Pu Taw's vision and task in action. It would provide a range of benefits for all parties and the Karen students would get out of the camp for an organised break which would give them plenty to talk about. And it worked. Youngsters who had spent years in the camps now had a taste of the wider world. Sports tournaments and cinema visits were organised; the Karen stayed in a hotel (a major first) and got lost in a shopping centre.

The Harrow youngsters visited migrant schools, spoke to local Burmese Community Based Organisations (notably one dealing with political prisoners) and met people whose experience was totally beyond the boundaries of their known world. A photographic project was a shared endeavour which highlighted how the Karen and Harrow students interpreted the world differently.

One 'cultural exchange' in particular stands out for me. It was organised for us by Greg Madden, an Australian whose huge enthusiasm and energy galvanised the whole weekend, and the delightful Yin, a Thai lady who worked as our logistics manager in Mae Sot. Harrow sent a very charming and able team, and the Karen youngsters were managed by the remarkable Som Boon, an urbane and kind man of middle years who suffered dreadfully with a hip problem which affected his mobility. He spoke almost fluent English and had converted to Christianity from Buddhism. He still seemed to hold to some semblance of Buddhist beliefs, putting his hip problem down to a wound he had suffered in a past life as a Karen soldier. It seemed pretty unfair in karmic terms, but Som Boon didn't complain. On this occasion, I had the opportunity to speak to a number of the Karen students about their lives, which I think are worth recounting, in some part, here.

Theh Dah Eh, twenty-two years old. She had spent the past twelve years in refugee camps. There had been much fighting in her area and her brother had been taken as a porter by the Burmese army. Her father was a target for special attention as he was a Karen soldier. The family had fled to Thailand.

Htoo Eh Thaw, twenty-four years old. She had spent eleven years in the refugee camps. Her father had died when she was young and when her mother married again, Htoo Eh Thaw and her brother had been sent to a camp, where they lived in a dormitory. She had eventually managed to get a place at PTMJC.

Heh Law La, twenty years old. His village had been attacked four times, so in 1995 the family had fled. Heh Law La had been brought up in refugee camps, where his father was a pastor and his mother a teacher.

These stories are typical and worth remembering in the light of what was shortly to follow. Despite a hard youth, these three young people remained positive, wanting to contribute to their communities in the future, and they would be needed. The Karen make light of hardship, and when the Harrow students departed Mae Sot airport to return to a very different world, the Karen group was there to see them off. I went to the airport to say my goodbyes, and as I approached the almost empty departure hall I could hear singing. This was the sound of real, unaccompanied voices, not the bland, piped sentimentality that breezes around most Thai public spaces. The Harrow team was making its way through baggage control and the Karen had formed a kind of choir. The young people from Harrow, now on their way back to an air-conditioned, high-tech First World, were being serenaded by youngsters who would soon be returning to the bamboo-and-wire confinement of a refugee camp. And what were the Karen singing to Harrow as they waved their goodbyes? The refrain was repeated over and over again without any intention of irony: "*Don't worry, be happy!*" It was a kind of emotional role reversal, with the Karen, eschewing any sense of victimhood, wishing goodwill to those who came from a much more privileged background. Leadership for a Better World. Pu Taw would have been proud of them, and Harrow would be prouder still, as we shall see.

Eighteen

The Lord of the Dance

Cosmic Dances, Pain and Gain, and the Return of the Princess, Mae Sot, Thai–Burmese Border, March 2015

You may know the figure of Shiva, the Nataraja, the Lord of the Dance, that wonderful, dynamic god who dances within a cosmic wheel of fire. He's a major Hindu deity and there's a massive statue of him at Rishikesh on the River Ganges, with which he is associated, but he has been appropriated by the rest of the world. He's very much a 'poster god', his image adding exotic ambience from New Age shops to Indian restaurants. Perhaps one of his biggest statues is, surprisingly, at the Hadron Collider at CERN in Switzerland. Shiva is a 'world god' as he represents the life force that is involved in a constant dance, destroying the old and bringing in the new. He's Hindu in origin but also Buddhist in the belief that all life is change, nothing is permanent. He's a hopeful figure, with one of his four hands gesturing peace, and a foot on a rather evil-looking creature which symbolises the ignorance he crushes. So in the figure we have dynamism, humanity and hope. It's an irresistible combination. And that brings us to the point. You can't escape change. It's how you handle it – or, rather, dance the difficult steps – that can cause problems. Shiva is well endowed with four arms and two muscular legs, but as mere mortals we have to do our best with what we've got. And therein lies the rub.

In 2015 the winds of change swept up the BEP, and Burma itself. I would like to call these 'periods of transition' but in both cases it was more seismic shock than any kind of gentle, butterfly-like metamorphosis. BEP had been doing a good job, in a rather informal, self-contained way. We had a team working on an English language project in the Karen refugee camps and we had a useful teacher-training project running in the migrant schools. We had already begun the process of change with the introduction of our first Burman and Karen staff and, as well as English, were delivering a course in Burmese language acquisition and teacher training. This was all manageable and well within our capacity. And then fate arrived in the form of the massive, international NGO Save the Children. Save the Children had been founded in 1919 by two remarkable sisters with deeply contrasting names: Eglantyne Jebb, whose name alone would ensure her a place in posterity, and the more prosaically named Dorothy Buxton. For almost one hundred years it had been involved in one humanitarian crisis after another from Europe to Ethiopia. It had now arrived on the Thai–Burmese border with a focus on, and money for, a teacher-training programme – or, more specifically, the development of teaching materials. BEP was offered the opportunity to run this one-year project. We would do the ground-level activities and World Education would look after the finances and some of the macromanagement. This would be our first major subcontract and would be rolled out in most of the seven camps along the border. So, in the spirit of Eglantyne and Dorothy, we decided to take it on.

Shiva's dance was now to have an effect on the whole organisation. We had an experienced team of Western trainers who would be responsible for this project, but they were used to a fairly informal way of operating. Over the years a quite relaxed way of life had become established and people enjoyed the working atmosphere, camaraderie and level of personal autonomy. Now something else was required: our elegant waltz would have to become a sharp military two-step. Two months into the project, things were not going well. I flew to Thailand and, having spent two weeks with the team, stayed on for another two. The team had worked together for almost two years, and roles and relationships were established. It was very difficult for them to readjust their egalitarian relationships into a more tiered structure to meet a very new situation. Leadership was an issue, with all that it meant for organisation and delegation. Any team needs a variety of players, and what we generally had was people who were used to taking on similar roles. That had been what was needed for previous projects, but this was different; a leader and organiser was needed now. The time I spent with the team at least got us moving to the same beat, but the rhythm was anything but smooth.

A few weeks later a new member, Eilish, joined the team, initially to take care of training in the humanities subjects.

Very shortly she realised that leadership was an issue and, as she had experience in this area, offered her services. Under the circumstances it was an offer we couldn't refuse. Eilish set the team on what was almost a business footing. A regime of strict office hours, report-writing, deadlines and the occasional dressing-down was introduced. Slowly and painfully a new working culture began to establish itself. In general, the team hated it and became increasingly hostile. Our priority in the UK was to complete the project as professionally as possible.

Sharp transition such as this is painful and, in hindsight, BEP UK should have brought in a project manager from the outside right at the beginning, but running with the team we had and monitoring from the UK, we did not realise how difficult it was for the existing team. Perhaps we just asked too much of them. Eilish led the dance but her strict approach created difficulties within the British team. On the one hand the team was unhappy, and on the other we had a manager who felt under threat and asked for support. We had to keep manager and team in place as it was the only way we could complete the project. Managing this from a distance was almost impossible. Chris Crick, one of the directors, and I spent hours on Skype trying to placate the team and keep the manager from resigning. Nevertheless, the project was completed with some success. A transformation had taken place and it was now up to us to make sure it continued, but in a somewhat different way. With that in mind, we appointed our first Burmese manager, Wai Mar Phyo, a young lady from Mandalay who had been with us for two years, and Emma Marsh, an experienced teacher from the UK, to work alongside her, supported by the equally experienced and very capable Alex Noyes, and a young intern from Durham University, Rob Whitelaw. Alex was devoted to her work and students in Mae La, and she and Rob got on very well. It was always something of a privilege bringing young interns into the team and watching them grow with the support of more experienced trainers. We also had a first-rate ally in Patrick Kearns, whom I mentioned earlier. He was now the new country director of World Education. This arrangement worked, and by September that year the team was settled and we were subcontracted for two more projects: a Literacy Boost project in the camps funded by Save the Children, and a teacher-training programme in the migrant schools as part of the Project for Local Empowerment (PLE) funded through World Education. In the next year we would win further contracts with Safe Child Thailand and, inside Burma, the Myanmar Education Consortium. We had survived the whirling dance of Shiva, any delusions we'd had had been crushed, and, life force intact, we began a new dance with much gusto. I'm sure Eglantyne and Dorothy would have been pleased.

Back at Coffee Corner, Phu had been insulted by Jesus. This contemporary namesake turned out to be a young American chap who during breakfast had become overzealous about his faith and told her she should burn her pictures of Hindu deities or suffer the hellish consequences. This had sent Phu into a karma-defying rage. Mae Sot seemed to attract the extremist wing of everything, as recounted earlier with the philanthropic fascists and others. And they continued to come, all certain of their calling. A Norwegian sniper, equipped with long-range sight, was set on butchering Burmese soldiers, and a Welsh wannabe mercenary asked me if I could speak English as, being too well groomed to be an Anglo-Saxon, he thought I was French. I took it as a compliment as he obviously thought the English to be sartorially limited. He finished up in much trouble after smashing up a bar one night. Another day a group of very earnest missionaries arrived wearing black ties and suits and talking very loudly about 'the mystery that is God', which brought an unsettling Old Testament feel to breakfast time. Dan had returned to Australia where, I heard, he was recuperating from the excesses of life on the border. I missed his good company and his stories.

Of more pressing concern had been a growing spate of small, ugly incidents in the town. One of our excellent staff, Andrea, had been mugged when riding home one night, and a good friend of mine, Phil Towns, had been set upon by a group of men with knives, but had stood his ground and seen them off. After that we all wanted T-shirts with Phil's face on them. The attacks stopped and things fell back to whatever passed as normal in Mae Sot.

The Thai border was always awash with rumours of spies and Burmese hit squads but this was all in the context of the political world. For us threats tended to take the form of attempted muggings. And this brings me to my own very personal brush with banditry.

I was travelling home from the border and staying in a small hotel. The rooms were comfortable and mosquito wire covered the windows. It was a hot, sticky night and I fell into a light sleep only to be woken by the sound of something clicking, followed by a silence. At times like these you really just want to go back to sleep so generally convince yourself that all is well and, in this case, it's probably a small gecko hunting on the window. But something did not seem quite gecko-like about that sound. In the pitch dark I fumbled for the bed-side light and grudgingly hauled myself out of bed. The room was empty, not even a gecko on the walls but, I noticed something; the wire of the mosquito screen was loose. Hesitantly, I walked to the end of the bed and suddenly froze. There, still as a corpse, on the floor was a man dressed all in black looking directly at me. Now, it's at this point that I feel I must add that if ever you find yourself in this unenviable position, that's mine, not that of the 'corpse', then you have nothing to worry about; even if you are sober. The body is a remarkable thing. It immediately takes over and you know exactly what to do. 'Know' is actually not the 'mot juste' here. There is nothing at all cerebral about what is to follow. You become someone or something else and you don't need that someone to negotiate terms by, perhaps, settling up with a small donation to the Burglars' Ball or to express a wish to understand the difficulties of a life of petty crime by asking, 'What's a nice chap like you doing breaking into hotel rooms and terrifying guests?' What you need is Clint Eastwood!

"I will kill you! Phom ja kar khun!" a voice began to shout. It was apparently me in 'Clint-mode' and in 'action-underwear'; snarling, fists raised, body rigid and totally alert and shouting in Thai and English, "I will kill you!!" Situations like this take you completely out of yourself. My body must have figured out in a micro-second that theatrical aggression was the best course of action.

It seriously bothered the 'corpse'. He jumped up, backed away and flattened himself against the wall. He was a Thai man of middle years, perhaps past his cat-burgling peak, tallish and of medium build wearing a black shirt and shorts. Thankfully, he had fear, or more dangerously, desperation, in his eyes and, as far as I could tell, he was unarmed.

He glanced at my wallet by the bed and there was a moment charged with tension. Would he try for it? Silence. Another glance. Tense silence. He was calculating his chances.

Clint, "I will kill you!"

Lazarus, "Sorry!"

And with another apology he fumbled open the door and ran into the night, and hopefully into early retirement.

The Thai police, in uniforms and plain clothes, eventually arrived mob-handed and bustled into the room. A young policewoman with an ipad decorated with a blue and pink bear took photos and joked that I might like a gun. She'd obviously bought into the Clint act.

Far from the low level banditry of the Thai border Shiva had been busy inside Burma addressing greater wrongs. On 8 November 2015, the Burmese world changed. A general election saw the NLD, under the leadership of Aung San Suu Kyi, affectionately known as Daw Suu (Mother/Lady Suu), win a landslide victory, taking eighty-six per cent of the seats. The military's proxy, the Union Solidarity and Development Party (USDP), was virtually wiped out. The country was ecstatic, and wild scenes of jubilation ensued in the streets of major cities and villages alike. The NLD's red and gold fighting peacock flag flew everywhere. The hated military had been roundly thrashed, and Daw Suu, the People's Princess, was transcendent. It was as if the old Burmese legend of the prince – or in this case princess –

in waiting, the Min Laung, had come true. The last time I had seen Aung San Suu Kyi had been in 1996 when, under house arrest, she had spoken to the crowds from her gate. It had been a moving moment, and now she was about to fulfil her destiny. Things appeared to be going in the right direction for Burma (or Myanmar, as it was now called). The generals even took to social media, looking metaphorically cool enough to reverse climate change. From their Facebook pages, the incumbent president and former general, Thein Sein, and the commander-in-chief of the Myanmar armed forces, Senior General Min Aung Hlaing, both congratulated Aung San Suu Kyi. There were promises that the Tatmadaw would cooperate with the new government following the transition.

Or so it seemed. For us, and for Burma, it was a 'Shiva moment'. In his eternal cosmic dance, the Nataraja had destroyed the old and brought in the new. We now began to move our projects inside Burma. In situations like this it's often prudent to stand back and take a moment to remind yourself of the Bard's message. Things are never quite what they appear to be.

Moving On

2016–2017

In 2016 the charity changed its name once again. We were the Burma Education Partnership, but Burma had changed its name to Myanmar, and we also sensed that we needed to give the organisation the room to expand if the opportunity came. We hit on the title Mobile Education Partnerships (MEP) and adopted a logo featuring the Greek Pegasus, representing learning and dynamism, and the lotus, an Eastern symbol of wisdom and enlightenment. We would need all of these qualities over the next couple of years.

Taking Stock

For Those Who Wish to Go Down This Path

Know your team and work within your capacity, but don't be afraid to take on a challenge. Be flexible and creative. All life is change.

Everyone carries 'baggage', and so do you. See if you can identify it before it gets you into the same trouble it has in the past.

Be prepared for Kipling's 'impostors', Triumph and Disaster. Be steady. Don't let either of the beasts carry you away.

And don't sing…

Nineteen

'Something is Rotten in the State of Denmark'[23]

Assassination, Fascist Monks and a Very Conflicted Lady, Burma 2015–17

On 29 January 2017 the lawyer and legal adviser to Aung San Suu Kyi, U Ko Ni, aged sixty-three, flew into Yangon airport. He was looking forward to being reunited with his family after a trip to Indonesia. On that hot afternoon he made his way through the crowds to the pavement outside the airport and was happy to see his family waiting for him. His last act was to scoop up his small grandson into his arms. A man in a pink shirt approached from behind and, raising a Czech-made nine-millimetre pistol, shot U Ko Ni in the back of the head. The grandson fell unscathed to the ground, which was now stained with his grandfather's

---

23   *Hamlet* by William Shakespeare, Act 1, Scene 4.

blood. Pursued by a mob, the assassin made off. More shots rang out and a taxi driver in the crowd was gunned down before the assassin was cornered and captured. What, then, had brought about this terrible scene which sent shock waves through the newly appointed government?

In order to understand this, we have to examine the Burmese constitution. Although this may sound a rather dry and legalistic undertaking, the constitution is a controversial and potentially explosive document which holds the fate of the nation in thrall. I will attempt to explain why. The 2008 constitution, written by the military, was a blatant piece of political chicanery. In the document, the military, in a moment of inspired self-interest, earmarked twenty-five per cent of the seats in all houses of the Burmese Parliament for themselves. They had no elections to win; the seats were theirs automatically. The genius of the arrangement goes further. Any changes to the constitution required backing from at least seventy-six per cent of the vote. The military's role was enshrined in the constitution for posterity. Further to that, the constitution gave them control over the key Ministries of Home, Border Affairs, and Defence. This had major implications, as we shall see. As a final poke in the eye for democracy, the military could also appoint one of the country's two vice presidents. They had the future sewn up... or so they thought.

If that wasn't enough to assuage the worries of a general suffering from creeping paranoia, then a bizarre clause was added. It stated that anyone who had children with foreign citizenship could not run for president. This was tantamount to an admission that the paranoia was now almost terminal, as the clause was targeted directly at Aung

San Suu Kyi, who had two sons to her British husband, both of whom had been born in Britain. This looked like the end of the game for The Lady. However, the generals hadn't reckoned on U Ko Ni's vast knowledge of the law. He found a way around the legal barrier to Aung San Suu Kyi taking power by identifying that a post of state counsellor could be created, which would be above that of president. Checkmate by The Lady. This move did not go down too well with those fearing an impending doomsday for their interests. In the shadows, figures considered their futures.

But even more threatening activity was under way. U Ko Ni was now focusing on the possibility of rewriting the constitution itself to remove the military's influence. This was in fact the reason for his trip to Indonesia, which he had visited with a party of Burmese officials and activists to look at ways in which governments can transition from military to civilian rule. This was dangerous territory. However, things could get even riskier as the group contained a number of Buddhists and Rohingya Muslims who would also address the issues of reconciliation between their communities in Rakhine State. And this brought into play another contentious issue: ethnicity and religion. U Ko Ni himself was a Muslim. As we will see, the country was now on the brink of a huge humanitarian crisis involving allegations of genocide.

From October 2016 to January 2017, the military had launched a crackdown on the Rohingya, a Muslim minority living in Rakhine State adjacent to Bangladesh. It is important to see the part the constitution played in this, as the military has, by law, control of the Ministries of Home, Border Affairs, and Defence. They can therefore act independently of the elected government. The Rohingya had suffered at the hands of various military governments over the years and in 2012 intercommunal tensions had flared up, leading to a hundred and forty thousand Rohingyas being resettled in IDP camps. They were still there in 2015. In 2016 things got worse. According to Burmese state sources, in October Rohingya militants attacked a Burmese police post, killing twelve officers. The Burmese military's response was draconian. In December Amnesty International reported extrajudicial killings, gang rapes, brutalities against civilians and looting. Human Rights Watch released satellite images of 5 burned villages containing 1,250 houses. On 3 February 2017 the Office of the UN High Commissioner for Human Rights reported 'massive and systematic' sexual violence against Rohingya women by the Burmese military. There was a mass exodus to the Bangladeshi border. But this was just the start, and, importantly, it was part of a much wider military offensive in which MEP would become involved.

Over the years this anti-Muslim sentiment had been fuelled by the most unlikely source of ethnic hatred: the Buddhist Sangha – or, to be exact, an organisation within the Sangha calling itself 969. As usual, numbers are not just digits in Burma; they have supernatural potency. In this case, the first 9 stands for the nine special qualities of the Buddha, the 6 for the six special elements of the Dharma, and the last 9 for the nine special attributes of the Sangha itself. But according to the writer Alex Bookbinder, this goes even further as supporters of 969 see in the use by Muslims of the number 786 (a numerical conversion of the words 'In the name of Allah, the compassionate, the merciful') a plot to take over the world in the twenty-first century, as these digits total twenty-one. The number 969 is a cosmic counter to this. Bizarre conspiracy theories are not confined to Trump's America! The 969ers were led by the monk Ashin Wirathu, who, despite protestations to the contrary, was seen by many as peddling anti-Muslim sentiment. The organisation ran a nationalistic campaign and called for a boycott of Muslim businesses. Eventually, in 2013, 969 left the cosmic battle and clearly stated its very worldly case, changing its name to the Association for the Protection of Race and Religion, or Ma Ba Tha (Country, Language, Religion). The now overtly nationalist group was successful in persuading President Thein Sein to approve four controversial laws concerning race and religion that imposed restrictions on interfaith marriage, birth spacing, polygamy and conversion. These laws were believed to be targeted at Muslims.[24] In 2014 anti-Muslim riots broke out in Mandalay. In a sinister twist, some observers believed that Ma Ba Tha was linked to the military.

The army began its attacks on the Rohingya in 2016, and in May 2017 Ma Ba Tha was involved in instigating anti-Rohingya riots in Yangon. Thankfully, the mainstream Buddhists, now under the incoming NLD government, were having none of this. In May 2017 the ruling body of the Sangha in Burma announced that Ma Ba Tha was an unlawful organisation and banned it from operating under its current name. Due to his use of hate speech, Wirathu was also banned from preaching for one year. But the nationalist monks were inventive. Wirathu continued

---

24   *The Irrawaddy*, 3rd September 2018.

to travel the country, broadcasting pre-recorded sermons with duct tape plastered across his mouth. Ma Ba Tha took to rebranding and came up with its next incarnation: the Buddha Dharma Charity Foundation. Peace and love were not top of its agenda.

This has taken us a little way from U Ko Ni's murder, but it is important to place it in its context and significance for what was to come. U Ko Ni's killer, Kyi Lin, a man with a criminal record, was sentenced to death. He always claimed to have acted under duress. A former military officer accused of hiring him, Aung Win Zaw, also received the death sentence. His brother, Aung Win Khine, who was accused of initiating the plot, was on the run. Significantly, Zeyar Phyo, another former military officer, received a five-year sentence for destroying evidence linked to the murder. So former military officers were clearly involved, but as always in Burma, the detail of the plot seems to disappear in the usual maze of smoke and mirrors. Ashin Wirathu publicly thanked the killer of U Ko Ni.

The anti-Rohingya virus was now abroad and infected public opinion. Creating a scapegoat, an enemy, a threat to the people is a well-used (and deadly) political trick; one that works time and time again in different forms. Once the virus is in the system it is difficult to remove. Many now saw Islam as a threat to national identity. Mutual distrust festered. What was to come was a nightmare. In August 2017, apparently in response to Arakan Rohingya Salvation Army attacks on border posts, the military launched an offensive against the Rohingya in Rakhine State. Estimates claim that around twenty-five thousand were killed and sexual violence perpetrated against eighteen thousand

Rohingya women. Nearly one million Rohingya fled to neighbouring Bangladesh for safety. It was the biggest refugee crisis since the Vietnam War. One of the main perpetrators of the violence was the 33rd Light Infantry Division, which would later play a role in MEP's story. The UN called this 'a textbook example of ethnic cleansing', and the following year the United Nations High Commission for Human Rights declared that the Burmese generals should be tried for genocide. Aung San Suu Kyi was criticised for not speaking out against the attacks, and later went to The Hague to answer criticism of the military. In her address to the International Court of Justice she claimed that although it could 'not be ruled out' that the Burmese military might have used 'disproportionate force' or 'did not distinguish clearly enough' between rebels and civilians, 'impatient international actors' gave the impression that 'only resource-rich countries can conduct adequate domestic investigation and prosecutions'. It seems almost unimaginable that Aung San Suu Kyi, who had opposed the military for so many years, who had won the Nobel Peace Prize in 1991, and who, over twenty years previously, I personally had heard speak against fascism to the Burmese people, could actually appear to be defending armed forces perpetrating such violence.

What, then, was going on? To a certain extent, I will have to leave this question to political analysts, and perhaps we will never know what was in The Lady's mind. One thing I will say is that it appears to me that Aung San Suu Kyi is her father's daughter. To revisit a little Burmese history, Aung San opposed the British and the Japanese and was the architect of independence, the father of the nation.

His vision was that of a Federal Union of Burma based on democratic principles which allowed for the political aspirations of ethnic groups. He was assassinated in 1947, six months before his first goal, independence, was realised. Like Hamlet, whose father was killed by his own brother, Aung San Suu Kyi is in many ways haunted by the ghost of her father. To continue the literary analogy, Aung San's vision of Burma was betrayed by his former brother-in-arms, Ne Win, who established a dictatorship rather than a democracy. Aung San Suu Kyi, I feel, is determined to fulfil her father's vision and will do whatever is necessary to achieve this.

One significant outcome of the whole business was that Aung San Suu Kyi's reputation was tarnished internationally. This could have huge implications for the future of democracy in the country. Despite international condemnation, she remained immensely popular amongst the Burmese people; arguably more so following her defence of the country at The Hague. Did she have a Hamlet 'To be, or not to be?' existential moment, asking herself:

Whether 'tis nobler in the mind to suffer
The slings and arrows of outrageous fortune,
Or to take arms against a sea of troubles,
And by opposing end them: to die [politically speaking –
My addition]?

Her decision to refrain from criticising the military must have been born out of the same kind of Hamlet-like vacillation. What would be the consequences of damning the military? What would be the consequences of defending them? How could she best take the country towards the elusive goal of democracy? How could she best follow her father? As always in Burma, the karmic forces of the past haunt the present. She had to be prepared for the 'slings and arrows' from the rest of the world, and to much of the world the decision she made compromised her morally. In Buddhist terms, however, this may be disputable. According to the Dharma, the moral assessment of an act depends on the intention behind it. One wonders if this had any bearing on her decision. We shall never know, but one is compelled to ask whose purposes the international vilification of Aung San Suu Kyi serves. We shall revisit this later. At this point a word of warning is perhaps prudent, as in Shakespeare's play, everyone ends up dead!

How, then, was MEP faring in 'Denmark'? Whatever was going on politically, we focused on the ordinary people caught up in it all. It was the safest route for us, and it worked. Our 2014 application to the Big Lottery UK for support for the MNEC project had been declined. A beast of a bid, it had consumed hours of work. Informing the Mon ladies had not been easy, and through our polite exchange of emails I'd felt their sense of disappointment bordering on rejection.

Nevertheless, by early 2017 we were working in Mon State, but with a different partner. This was thanks to the efforts of a Burmese girl who was not hanging around Kipling's pagoda, but part of our team. Wai Mar Phyo was from Mandalay, which would have pleased the poet, and her father had worked for the Burmese successor to the Irrawaddy Flotilla Company celebrated in Kipling's poem. Over two to three years, MEP had gradually brought more and more local trainers into its team, and now operated with only a small number of Westerners. Wai Mar Phyo had been our team leader in Mae Sot and had now moved back over the border and established our first Burma-based project. We had an office in Moulmein and were officially registered to work in Mon State. Our project focused on a neglected area of Mon education: the *pongyi jaun*, or monastic schools.

Monastic education dates back to at least the eleventh century and for hundreds of years was the main provider of education, contributing to the very high Burmese literacy rate in the early to mid-twentieth century. Currently, monastic schools provide education for orphans and the children of needy families. As well as instruction in the Buddhist faith and ethics, a variety of subjects are taught. One thing the teachers often lacked was sufficient training. This was certainly our area, and, using Burmese trainers who had experience of working with us in Thailand, Wai Mar Phyo set up a mobile training unit to work initially with eleven schools, with the main training centre at Dahmathuka school. It was a system we had employed very successfully in the migrant and refugee schools of the Thai border, and now we could establish the same system within Burma. Many of the pupils came from internally displaced or internal migrant families. Some had moved away from border areas, fearing that they would be used as porters by armed groups and their children taken as child soldiers. Many had moved for economic reasons, joining the labourers on the rubber plantations providing Burma with 'white gold'. We now even had a Burmese advisory board incorporating members from the NLD's education wing, education advisers, and a principal of a school working with street children in Yangon. Our first project lasted from May to October 2017, during which time we delivered training to one hundred teachers.

With our Burmese team and office inside the country we were making our own transition and looking forward to the future. Our brief was to work with marginalised communities, and in reality this meant those suffering from the effects of war, displacement and poverty. There were many such in Burma. The situation of the Rohingya was desperate. However, they were not the only people suffering from the depredations of the military. In late September 2017 a seven-member panel of the independent and influential Permanent Peoples' Tribunal found the Burmese military guilty of genocide against the Rohingya and 'Kachin minority groups'. Our work was now to take us into the far north of Burma in support of the Kachin; a people who for many years had been fighting for a level of autonomy. Kachin State was held partly by the rebels and partly by the Burmese army. It was to be one of the most remarkable projects we had ever undertaken.

Twenty

The Sword of Gideon

Jealous Gods, the Front Line and Kachin 101, Kachin State, Northern Burma, December 2016

> *During that night the LORD said to Gideon, "Get up, go down against the camp, because I am going to give it into your hands…". Grasping the torches in their left hands and holding in their right hands the trumpets they were to blow, they shouted, "A sword for the LORD and for Gideon!" While each man held his position around the camp, all the Midianites ran, crying out as they fled.*
> (Judges, 7:15–20)

Around 10am on 11 December 2016, two plumes of smoke rose out of the jungle covering the ridge known as Gideon Boom (Gideon's Hill). The Burmese army had begun a bombardment which would continue for another four hours with around seventy-five mortar rounds pounding the maze of trenches, underground bunkers and tunnels on the spine of the ridge occupied by the Kachin forces. Gideon's Hill was a key position defending a main route through Kachin State, and its loss would be a blow to Kachin morale and their whole movement. It could also open the way for the Burmese army to launch an assault on the Kachin capital of Laiza. Why, then, was this Gideon's Hill?

The Kachin are in the main Christian Baptists, while the rest of Burma is principally Buddhist. Biblical reasons for the name of the hill made good sense in the Kachin universe. With limited forces and facing overwhelming odds, for many years the Kachin had been fighting a war for self-determination against the military dictatorship. Old Testament stories of small forces defeating vast hosts therefore went down well. In case you have forgotten the story of Gideon since your Sunday-school days, let me refresh your memory. Gideon, now a rather obscure but colourful figure found in the depths of the Old Testament, was a warrior king of some renown and a big favourite with the Kachin; a kind of Bronze Age superhero. His sworn enemies were the Midianites, who brought a great host against him. Unfazed, Gideon considered his options. The traditional god of many of the Israelites was Baal, but Jehovah was a contender. Caught in the divine power struggle, Gideon needed the right god to believe in, and asked Jehovah for help. He, rather counter-intuitively, told Gideon to reduce his army from an unlikely twenty-two thousand to a much smaller force. This downsizing would demonstrate that the coming victory would be attributable to the power of Jehovah rather than the size of the army. Divine self-interest is a potent force, and Gideon, who obviously enjoyed taking risks, agreed. The selection process bears some examination. The army was taken to a river and told to drink. Those who knelt and drank directly from the river were rejected, but those who lapped the water like a dog from their cupped hands were selected. The reasoning behind this is, to say the least, obscure or part of some arcane bush lore. However, the water test left Gideon with a mobile unit of 300 who duly thrashed the Midianites. Notably, scare tactics were used as Gideon's commandos attacked, blowing trumpets, hurling burning jars of oil and shouting the war cry, "A sword for the Lord and for Gideon!" Equally notably, it was the Kachin 252nd Mobile Battalion now sitting on that ridge being bombarded by the new-look Midianites. Holding that hill, as we will see, would be important to MEP. I'm not sure how the 252nd were drinking their water.

A month earlier in November 2016 I had crossed from China into the rebel-held area of Kachin State. It was impossible to do this from the Burmese side as Westerners were banned from entering the area controlled by the Kachin Independence Organisation (KIO). The KIO had been fighting the military dictatorship since the 1960s, and despite a seventeen-year ceasefire the fighting had kicked off again in 2011. In general, the Burmese army controlled the major towns, but the Kachin Independence Army (KIA) seemed to hold sway in tracts of mountainous, jungle-covered terrain. The area is rich in jade. In fact, in the middle of the capital, Myitkyina, instead of the usual statue of a local hero there is a huge chunk of green jade (or a lookalike) on a plinth. The jade mines of Hpakant were much fought over by the Kachin and the Burmese and the industry is reputedly worth $30 billion annually. How much of that gets to the young men and women drawn here is disputable. Conditions for many 'miners' are reminiscent of the Klondike, with thousands of young people racing on motorcycles along the edges of the huge grey crater to stake a claim, or on foot to be first to scavenge amongst the loads of waste dumped by the mining trucks. It's a grim sight, and fatalities are high.

The Kachin, like the Karen, had been great friends of the British and had formed the 101 Kachin Rifles fighting alongside them and Frank Merrill's American forces against the Japanese in World War II. The number 101 came to be associated with being a 'real' Kachin, and I saw it inked onto the spines of workbooks possessed by many Kachin students. Numbers, as we have seen, are important in Burma, as they are sometimes infused with supernatural powers.

Newly rebranded as Mobile Education Partnerships, we had been invited into the KIO-controlled area by an old friend of mine, Khun Seng Lahpai, who I had met when he was a student at Newcastle University. Khun Seng was now the head of the Mai Ja Yang Institute of Education situated just over the Chinese border inside Burma. The institute drew students from all over Kachin State and produced qualified teachers, but there was one thing they needed and valued: an internationally recognised certificate. As much of their course was delivered in English, this was where we could be useful. We had experience of delivering Cambridge English language courses leading to certificates accredited by Cambridge Assessment. We had managed to secure a grant, which allowed us to send two teachers to Mai Ja Yang. Rob Gordon, a former head teacher from Bristol, assisted by his teaching partner Ann Pearce, would deliver the course. This was a huge opportunity for the students and a huge risk for us, as the KIO area was out of bounds to Westerners and there was no way into the area through Burma. It had, in fact, taken some negotiations to get our teachers into Kachin State by the back door over the Chinese–Burmese border.

Built primarily to create a gambling resort for rich Chinese, Mai Ja Yang was now really an education centre for the Kachin, with schools and colleges blossoming around the town as the old casinos were boarded up. Khun Seng had fixed the entry over the border with the Chinese, and we drove into Mai Ja Yang without meeting a checkpoint. To say the least, Khun Seng's college was impressive. The imposing architecture had almost a neoclassical feel about it and the surrounding grounds were well tended. Bungalows with cooking facilities in an adjoining annex were available for guests. Everything in Burma has to begin with a ceremony, and within fifteen minutes of reaching Mai Ja Yang I was standing in front of Kachin students and teachers giving something of a speech. A small piece of advice here: never attend a Burmese function empty-handed. Not having a gift can cause you much embarrassment. A picture of Durham Cathedral is a guaranteed face-saver and, with something of a flourish, I produced one from my luggage. However, this was nothing compared to the splendid response by the Kachin. A young man approached me carrying a magnificent *dah*, a Kachin sword, with white scabbard decorated with the red and green of the Kachin flag. Drawing the blade from the scabbard and running my thumb along the edge, I was completely smitten. It made my painting of Durham Cathedral feel like a Christmas card. This was a sword good enough for Gideon. She was totally seductive and beguiling and, like a femme fatale, could land me in a lot of trouble, which, as I will recount later, she duly did. Formalities over, we got down to the real business of consuming significant quantities of the excellent Kachin rice wine; a serious home brew poured from plastic bottles. It is quite a potent drink, and the best head-fuddling brew I ever tasted was, surprisingly, purple in colour. The sale of alcohol is illegal in the KIO area of Kachin State!

It was now three months into the course, which was scheduled to run until February 2017 when the exams would be delivered. The college had tried to make Rob and Ann as comfortable as possible. However, isolation was a problem. This hadn't stopped them doing a marvellous job with the students; introducing new teaching techniques; designing teaching aids with low-cost materials (a necessary skill if the young teachers were to work in rural areas); using the classroom walls to display posters, signs, key vocabulary and language tips; and generally bringing in the outside world. Many rural schools had none of this and were drab structures which could have been brought to life with a few simple ideas to create a learning environment. The Kachin students were brimming with enthusiasm and had even designed their own uniform for the course, with a logo displaying crossed *dahs* as a centrepiece for the text 'Kachin Cambridge Course'. They held all the promise and energy of youth. Gideon would have recruited them all without the water test. Everything was on target for the exams in

February. All that was required was that the Midianites were kept at the foot of the hill.

Over the next couple of days, we visited schools and camps for IDPs. The war had created a serious displacement problem amongst civilians. They had not fled across the porous Chinese border, but 100,000 of them were now in 138 camps located right on the border and around the state. It was a repetition of the human tragedy I had seen twenty years ago on the Thai border. The same drama was being played out here. The Kachin essentially wanted their own state as part of a federal union, but they wanted to run the show themselves as they feared that the large Burmese population would take control and they would be no further forward. It was a kind of ethnic nationalism; difficult to accept in purist liberal democratic terms but understandable given the history of the country. The KIA, estimated at perhaps four thousand active troops, controlled strips of the country with a brigade allocated to each KIA-controlled area. There were five brigades, with a sixth being the mobile brigade sent to areas which needed support. KIA 3rd Brigade was stationed at Mai Ja Yang. The nights were bitterly cold, and in the darkness the sound of automatic weapon fire could be heard from the high ground to the north. It was a sobering reminder that this was the edge of a war zone, and over the next few days we were to see more of this.

Khun Seng had arranged a trip to Laiza and we left bright and early in four-wheel drives, moving off the tarmac and onto the old British-made Burma Road (there are several) heading north. The scenery is spectacular, with the yellow road leading into the vast, verdant and mountainous landscape. To our right, just inside China, the paddy fields of Yunnan Province spread to the far blue mountains. We clattered across the wooden slats of the Ta Ho River Bridge and stopped at a checkpoint manned by three quite relaxed KIA soldiers. The checkpoint displayed a strange assortment of what appeared to be rusting, pineapple-shaped landmines; these served as a grim warning regarding the area we were about to enter. Pulling out of the Ta Ho Valley, the front line of the conflict began to reveal itself. The Kachin held the high ground with a system of trenches and bunkers linking one hill to the next. Each brigade controlled twenty posts, assigning fifteen to twenty men to each.

We stopped for lunch at one such post, located on the side of a ridge overlooking a steep river valley. Two bamboo huts were the only presence above ground. Not really knowing what to make of our intrusion, a couple of young soldiers in fatigues and flip-flops stood around half smiling, half wondering. Dishevelled hair and rather bleary eyes seemed to suggest we had woken them from a midday snooze. Nevertheless, the red crossed swords on their shoulder flashes supported my Old Testament theory. They propped their weapons casually against the bamboo wall and watched as a lady served us some noodles and then went back to sewing a shirt. The noodles, although cold and greasy, were much preferable to the roasted monkey's feet we had been offered at a post earlier in the day. Chickens scratched around and two rather mangy puppies scampered up to see us and, finding little to their interest, scurried back into the dusty shade. Plastic bags full of water, used to extinguish flash fires, hung from the bamboo eaves like shabby Christmas decorations. Sitting temptingly on a bench was a large box containing bottles of Chinese Harbin beer. The label showed snowy mountain peaks against the golden coolness of the beer. It was almost too much to endure in the baking heat. Outside, trenches snaked away to bunker after bunker. In the monsoon this place would look like something from my grandfather's war in Flanders. Deep in the valley at a distance of about 200 yards were other positions. These were manned by the Burmese. A sense of ennui hung over everything and I wondered who really wanted to die defending this ridge. Better to share a Harbin beer or two. This illusion was soon to be shattered by the attack on nearby Gideon Boom, where, I was told, only sixty metres divided the opposing lines.

We continued to follow the road cut through by the British in World War II to supply Chiang Kai-shek's Kuomintang in Yunnan Province. One reflects on the layer upon layer of struggle in this region as armies came and went across the porous borders. Some of the great games of history had been played out in this remote area. The British, the Japanese, the Americans, the Kuomintang and the communists had all struggled over this beautiful country. No wonder the Kachin wanted the place to themselves. Reaching a viewpoint just before Laiza, we stopped to eat. What followed was as much an experience as it was a meal. The Kachin accompanying us were only carrying rice wrapped in banana leaves and some soya beans and, of course, about two gallons of rice wine. Armed with knives, two young members of the group jumped from the vehicle and disappeared into the bush, scaling the jungle-covered side of the hill that rose above the road. Meanwhile, a fire was started, and a large pan of water brought to boiling point in time for the return of the gatherers, who brought with them an array of plants, all of which looked the same to me but which had obviously been selected with great skill. They were thrown quickly into the boiling water. Cups for the rice wine were skilfully fashioned from bamboo nodes sharpened at one end so they could be spiked into the ground. Everyone was given a banana-leaf plate, and very shortly we were absorbed in a meal of boiled rice and assorted jungle vegetables spiced with soya beans. It struck me that by carrying a little rice for substance the Kachin could, more or less, live off the land. We could travel the length of China with this team. The general bonhomie, good food and rice wine soon had me feeling like a 101 Kachin. Another node or two of the wine and I would have signed up for the KIA – well, maybe a staff job. I still prize that bamboo cup.

Later that day we rumbled quite merrily into Laiza, the rebel capital off limits to foreigners. It is quite a smart town, and a room at the excellent Laiza Hotel made a comfortable base for a couple of days. We were mainly interested in looking at the possibility of providing some kind of educational support in the IDP camps around the town. Jay Yang was the largest, with a population of about thirty thousand. Displacement in Burma is one of its greatest tragedies, especially if it is long term. Many of the IDPs scattered in the 138 camps around Kachin State reported human trafficking, especially out of the KIA area near the Chinese border. IDPs were making the risky journey across the border to find work and ending up being trafficked. A press release by the Myanmar government in 2016[25] claimed that up to fifty per cent of IDPs from the KIO-controlled area were on a daily basis crossing the border to find work in the coffee, banana and farming plantations. The report tells the story of one of two girls trafficked in 2011:

They said she would be looking after children. They brought her [to China] saying she would be paid 300 yuan a month, but she was sold to a rich Chinese man for 23,000 yuan instead. She gave birth to two children with this man and they forced her to work all day long. In the end, she managed to escape and return to the IDP camp.

Further to that, IDPs, with good reason, feared losing their traditional village land. The Durable Peace Programme (a consortium of seven international and local stakeholders) reported concerns that land belonging to IDPs was being appropriated by companies, other villages and 'armed actors'.[26] Some land was being used for mining and some for extensive plantations.

The IDP camps themselves were never completely safe. A 2017 Amnesty report described serious incidents in December 2016 when mortar and artillery shells landed near IDP camps in KIA-controlled areas, instilling fear in the people. Although there were KIA bases in the area, military experts:

---

25 Posted on ReliefWeb, 20th June 2016.
26 Durable Peace Programme Displaced and Dispossessed in Kachin State Report May 2018

*...believed the Myanmar Army's shelling was
likely unlawful, given the risk to a large number
of civilians and the failure to take measures... that
would have reduced the possibility of an overshot
that might land in the IDP camp.*

The report goes on to quote Dashi Hkawn Nu, a fifty-six-year-old woman with four children:

*"I was in my shelter. The whole family was there.
When the firing stopped, we managed to run... The
shells, one would land, then five minutes [of silence],
then another, then five minutes. It was so many
times. Even those [that exploded] far away, we could
hear them. We were very scared, we wanted to flee.
The ground was shaking. The sound, it was like it
was thundering."*

To make matters worse, there were reports of IDPs trying to cross into China for safety and then being pushed back.

At Jay Yang camp, situated in a rocky valley outside Laiza, I spoke to the headmistress of one school. Nang Aung Ni Shi was a bright, dedicated young lady but her description of the situation revealed a deep sense of frustration at the desperate conditions. The school catered for a huge intake of 1,875 children from Grades 1 to 8, and had 95 teachers. Parents of families coming in from rural areas knew little about education, and the difficulties of the situation made survival a priority. Parents crossed the border on a daily basis to find work. With no one at home, children might come into school, but often older children had to look after their younger siblings. It was common for children to be left alone at night if their parents did not return. Dropout began at thirteen or fourteen years of age.

Given the enormity of the circumstances our efforts seemed small indeed, but in time we began to bring IDPs into our Kachin State teacher-training programme. We were particularly pleased with this achievement. I put some of the success down to a meeting with Khun Nong, the KIO's education secretary. When I found out that his dog was called Wayne Rooney I knew we were on to a winner.

In Laiza the day ends as it starts: with a bugle call. It's a reminder of the Kachin struggle, and as the 'Last Post' is sounded, the ghosts of Empire seem to stir. The past, as always, feeds karmically into the present, even in Old Testament territory. We took a different road on the way back, past a checkpoint with young soldiers looking rather edgy. There was tension in the air; possibly the situation on Gideon's Hill was growing desperate. However, later that day the balance of military ennui and tedium was restored as we stopped at the post held by the 15th Battalion of the 3rd Brigade on the Ta Ho River. Captain Dum Daw Gram Seng had eschewed the olive green of the KIA and was into his 'alter ego'. Wearing the red-and-white stripes of Atlético Madrid, he sat in the shade and explained the situation. He had been stationed here for five months and had been a soldier in the KIA for sixteen years. He only managed to obtain leave to see his family once a year, if he had permission. This seemed to contrast with the situation for the nearby Burmese troops, who, he explained, were replaced on a rota, with fresh troops coming up every six months. He told me that recent air strikes at Gideon's Hill had killed two or three KIA troops, but in return a major and two captains of the Burmese army had lost their lives. It all seemed like a kind of bloody chess game in the mountains, with one side gaining advantage over the other according to which jungle-covered ridge gave them dominance. The latest phase of the war had dragged on for seven years. Captain Dum Daw Gram Seng did not know what he would do when he left the army. Of course, the grim caveat to that was '…if he survived that long'. While we were talking, an old man wearing military fatigues and carrying a short sword arrived, squatted down beside us and lit a cheroot. He introduced himself as Dim Mai, sixty-two years old and a former KIA soldier. He had walked all day from his village to visit his family in the IDP camp at nearby Dum Boom. We sat in silence and the bleakness of the situation hit me – here was a tableau of Kachin history: two soldiers whose lives spanned two generations of struggle, and a family languishing in an IDP camp. The captain's football shirt now seemed less an intrusion and more the embodiment of an aspiration for something better.

A few miles further along the road a white skull painted on a blue signboard, like some tribal fetish, warned us of mines in the area. Just as we arrived in the one street of Kom Ba village, a truck carrying about thirty soldiers of the KIA 3rd Brigade accompanied by others on motorcycles pulled to a dusty halt. The young men clambered down from the truck. A few of the locals sitting on their verandas smiled and waved. The unit was well equipped and smartly turned out in what appeared to be olive-green dress uniforms and large Chinese-style caps. They were in good spirits, smiled and posed for photos, and looked prepared more for a parade than for a spell in the trenches on the ridge. Notably, the officers carried black-handled swords in bamboo scabbards, their shoulder flashes displayed crossed swords, and, although lacking trumpets and oil jars, they sipped water, albeit from plastic bottles. Clearly they were Gideon's men.

Two days later I was on my way home, riding in the back of a four-wheel drive, with two of our Kachin students as driver and guide. It was a fresh morning as we drove through the rice paddies of Yunnan Province and passed old villages with high surrounding walls daubed with huge red Chinese lettering. It was the back way over the border; we were in good spirits and didn't expect to be stopped, but suddenly the mood changed as we were flagged down by uniformed men. If you have never had this experience then let me assure you it's all a bit melodramatic and downright undignified trying to make yourself unnoticeable in the back of a vehicle. It's also hopeless. The more inconspicuous you try to make yourself, the more obviously guilty of something you will appear. The two boys were taken away. An officer peered in the back window, looked straight at me, hesitated for ten quickening heartbeats and then walked smartly away. After a few minutes the young men returned looking rather disgruntled. They had had to give a urine sample for a drugs test. That is arguably more undignified than hiding in the back seat of a car. But more was to come.

The boys dropped me off at Mangshi airport and left quickly. At the check-in a rather expressionless young lady took my passport and signalled to me to put my luggage on the scanner belt. Her blank expression slowly transformed into a startled one as the scan image became clear. Checking the English on her translator app, she said, "Sir, you have knife in your case," and reached for a phone. There are moments when travelling when one faces tense apprehension. This is, in fact, a precursor to full-blown panic. It may spur you to flight, or something deeply primordial may take over and a resigned numbness grip your body. It's rather like standing outside the headmaster's office waiting for the industrial-level canings handed out when I was a boy.

Two police arrived and told me to open the case. The Chinese in the queue stared quietly, obviously relishing the whole business. It was rather like having a urine test in public. I fumbled for the keys and, after several tries, the cheap lock clicked open. From the crumpled clothes, like Excalibur, the Kachin sword in its white scabbard with red-and-green lanyard appeared. The queue loved it, and much sucking of breath and chattering ensued. Divine intervention was out of the question in a communist country and one of the officers took my prize away to an unknown fate while I was escorted to an equally unknown fate at the airport police station. I wondered if they had a copy of the Old Testament.

Between drags on a cigarette, an officer spoke sharply to me and then held up a mobile phone screen. The translator app stated, 'Exporting tools from China is illegal'. Although reality lost something in the translation, I got the drift. A smartly uniformed young lady appeared and started to question me in English while multiple copies of my passport were taken by her chain-smoking colleague. Where had I been? Mangshi? How had I obtained the sword? From a friend? Then where was the friend? I didn't know? Where did he live? If you are not used to lying then a little practice to prepare yourself for such situations is advisable – and stick to your story. Much signing of papers followed. I had no idea what they said. Maybe I had signed a confession. Maybe I would be 're-educated'. It was not exactly like something from *The Manchurian Candidate* but the enormity of the consequences if the truth were discovered did bring on a rather tepid sweat. There would be consequences for someone; maybe the two young men now driving on a back road through the rice paddies to Mai Ja Yang. There would be questions about how a Westerner had crossed that border; about my arrangement with the Kachin and who was involved. Eventually, I was allowed to leave, and then a most peculiar thing happened. The smart English-speaking young lady gave me her name and phone number so that when I was back in China I could collect my sword! I was astounded by her apparent largesse. If I'd been younger I might have read this differently, but the charms of an older man are not to be underestimated. I might give her a ring should the opportunity arise. But, come to think of it, she probably sold it on eBay.

Two weeks later I was back in England, reflecting on the odd behaviour of the Chinese police as well as my own stupidity, and staring at the blank space on the wall of my office where the sword should have been hanging. Chris Crick, who had also visited Kachin State, and I kept in touch with Rob and Ann as best as we could. One evening a text from Rob arrived with the disturbing news that the Burmese army had launched an offensive and was moving towards Mai Ja Yang. I checked the news from Burma. Our worst fears had come true. The loss of the sword had clearly been an omen. The Midianites had taken the hitherto impregnable Gideon's Hill. It had fallen after an aerial bombardment had smashed the defences and a subsequent infantry assault had swept away any remaining resistance. The carnage in those confined bunkers and trenches must have been horrific, and as the Burmese advanced I wondered if any of the casualties had been found in possession of a red-and-white striped football shirt. Had Captain Dum Daw Gram Seng survived to enjoy his well-earned leave? Our whole project was now in jeopardy and Rob and Ann's safety was compromised. Via Skype, Chris and I mentally paced the room and pondered all the options, but in effect we had no choice. We had to get Rob and Ann out quickly. Our decision would unleash a chain of events which would involve high tension, much goodwill, and great good fortune. But Gideon would prevail.

Twenty-one

Shooting the Stars,

Bunkers, Checkpoints and Johnny Depp
Kachin State, December 2016–February 2017

The sound of small-arms fire was part of the soundtrack of life in Mai Ja Yang, but one night this became massive explosions. Artillery fire could be heard south of the golf course. The eighteen-hole course had been built for the Chinese coming to gamble in the town's now-closed casinos. Under the current circumstances its bunkers could soon serve a different purpose. The notorious Burmese 33rd Light Infantry Division (the following year to be involved in the atrocities committed against the Rohingya) had clashed earlier in the month with the KIA's 17th Battalion between Muse and Namhkam just south of Mai Ja Yang. The fighting was moving closer. The road south was blocked, and Burmese positions were visible on the southern ridge overlooking the town. This meant that they could be advancing from two directions: from Gideon Hill in the north and Muse in the south. No one was on the golf course.

The usually sleepy town of Mai Ja Yang was a frenzy of activity. Digging trenches and distributing arms were top of the agenda. A new consignment of Kachin-made rifles had arrived at the KIA's 3rd Brigade HQ and been issued to every male, including our students. Training of sorts for the general populace was under way. This meant our students were woken at 5.30am by a bugler playing 'Reveille' and were soon out to join 'GI jogging sessions' with the 3rd Brigade. So, our Cambridge class was now armed and fitter. They arrived hot and sweating, but without rifles, to their early-morning English class. To be clear, some were already in the KIA, so this was not totally new to them. One of the teachers, Paul, was a captain in the KIA. He was one of six brothers, four of whom had already been killed in action, and the fifth had advised him to stick with his teaching. Six months later the fifth brother was killed. The town was on a war footing. Christmas lights were banned, and a kind of blackout imposed with power cuts at night. All the doctors and medical assistants had left for the front, and local women stockpiled as much wood as possible to keep fires going in the event of the electricity being cut off. The Manau Festival, a Kachin celebration on New Year's Eve involving traditional dancing and music, was cancelled.

Rob and Ann prepared to leave, but with the intention to return in a few weeks once the offensive was over. This was a terrible blow to the class as exams were scheduled for February and a gap in teaching would be a serious setback. The Kachin are an enormously cheerful and optimistic people, but this hit them hard. The possibility that Western teachers would again deliver an internationally accredited English course in war-torn Kachin State was, to say the least, remote. This was a first for them and for us, and for Rob and Ann the decision was heartbreaking after the effort they'd put into teaching and the relationships they'd built with the students, and with the possibility of success now in sight. Nevertheless, they put together a learning pack for the students to be used during the interim period and established WhatsApp groups so that they could monitor and mark work. This would at least maintain momentum and focus.

However, despite the approach of the Burmese, one quite fitting tradition remained: shooting stars, or rather, shooting *at* stars. In the cold of New Year's Eve, Rob and Ann were summoned to a gathering around a bonfire. Wrapped in coats, hats and scarves, eyes smarting from the smoke, they were provided with the usual half-gallon of rice wine, but this time accompanied by a rifle. The custom at midnight was to open fire on the stars shining in the clear night air. Singing 'Auld Lang Syne' seemed tame in comparison, and even the north-east custom of first footing, wherein local inebriates call in for a drink and bring a lump of coal and a silver coin for luck, seemed oddly quaint compared to blasting into the cosmos with an automatic weapon. I could see this catching on in parts of Sunderland. But why would anyone want to engage in such an activity? The explanation was that it was an attempt to shoot down the evil spirits of the incoming year. This was a leftover from pre-Christian animism, and great fun as well as a warning to the Burmese. I expect the Kachin hoped that Rob's aim was good, as evil spirits of another sort were now encircling the town.

The next day Rob and Ann left Mai Ja Yang on a circuitous route over the Chinese border and on to safety in Thailand. A week later, in a small hotel in Bangkok one thousand miles away from war-torn Kachin State, they contemplated their rapidly diminishing options. They wanted to return: this was a valuable certificate for the students, time was ticking away and the possibilities of delivering an exam were becoming slimmer. The key to success was to return in time to prepare the students for the exam and, of course, ensure the safe passage of the examiners into Mai Ja Yang. And who were the intrepid examiners willing to undertake such an unusual mission? Our old friends who worked with us every year in the refugee camps of the Thai border. Two of the original team, David Eastgate and Dava Romyanond, survivors of the first 'cassowary exams', were willing to deliver the exam but this time in a strictly freelance capacity. That was before the Burmese army, on their dry-season offensive, arrived at the golf course at Mai Ja Yang. The offensive posed huge difficulties. Access would be compromised. We needed a Plan B at least, and a lot of imagination.

But what was Plan B? Someone came up with the idea of delivering the exam across the Chinese border in the town of Ruili. This held much promise, and spirits rose. The idea was floated with Cambridge, who regrettably had to turn it down as, amongst a range of problems, there was not enough time to register an exam centre in Ruili. Hopes rather dented, we came up with Plan C. The exams could be postponed until March and hopefully the situation would have improved by then. Maybe Gideon's men would prevail and the Burmese would go home.

Wishful thinking indeed. This proposal crashed when the examining team said they were fully booked for March. Out of the ashes, Plan D began to form. Technology was the answer! Rob and Ann would download the exam onto their laptop, load it onto the college computers and do the invigilation themselves. Sadly (or not), humans are the curse of freewheeling technology. That option short-circuited when we discovered that we would still need a 'live examiner' to deliver the oral component. This couldn't be done remotely. The limitations of a technological rescue created frustration and led to creeping despondency. And then another potentially viable possibility presented itself. Plan E was a long shot and depended on humans, which is always a risk. The suggestion was to set up the exam in Myitkyina, the state capital. It was seven hours' drive away and there would be Burmese army roadblocks to negotiate, but it was safe and, although overland travel by foreigners was not allowed, there were flights. Plan E was a logistical nightmare but there was just a chance that it would work. The examiners with the Cambridge papers could reach Myitkyina in one day via two flights. Rob and Ann faced an exhausting journey: two hours by road from Mai Ja Yang followed by four flights over two days to reach Myitkyina in a roundabout trip through China, Thailand and Burma. Crossing borders would require visas. However, these difficulties were nothing compared with getting thirty-seven students by road from a no-go war-torn area to the state capital controlled by the enemy which had just threatened their well-being (and damaged the golf course) in Mai Ja Yang. One couldn't ignore the irony. Paperwork was required, which can be the kiss of death in Burma.

The students would need Burmese ID cards. Sadly, and rather peculiarly, this excluded five of the group who did not possess such documents and one pulled out, apparently for work-related reasons. The remaining exam candidates faced a seven-hour car journey across the front line and through three army checkpoints. It was doable.

With Plan E agreed with Khun Seng, Rob and Ann returned from Bangkok by the back door. With only two and a half weeks to prepare the students for the exams, extra lessons were arranged every day, Rob and Ann made themselves available at all hours, and the students took advantage of drop-in lessons over the weekends. At last, two days before leaving for Myitkyina, everything was ready. Then the clock stopped! It was Saturday night, and the students were watching their favourite film, *Pirates of the Caribbean*. Johnny Depp overcoming the might of the British navy and assorted socially inadequate villains has international appeal but reaches almost Old Testament status for a people fighting for their own cultural survival. Captain Jack was straight out of Deuteronomy. But now dark forces began to threaten. Rob's phone bleeped. It was a text from Dava. The words were blunt and their message shocking:

Disaster – Cambridge can't get the exam papers to us.

The beast of bureaucracy was upon us and Plan E was cursed. Even Johnny Depp looked like he would finish on the end of a rope. How to explain this crushing news to the students? It was unjust, it was cruel, but sadly, in these circumstances, it was life. The grimness of the disappointment hung like a gibbet. However, a buccaneering spirit was not confined to Hollywood pirates. Rob's phone bleeped again:

Hang on. David is on to them!

In swashbuckling style, on hearing the news David Eastgate had pulled his car to a halt, jumped out and, via his mobile, blasted some poor Cambridge official with a broadside. Cambridge quickly arranged for the papers to be emailed to us, along with a special password which would allow David and his loyal crew access. Plan E was now under full sail.

The whole operation required precise coordination and was fraught with difficulties. Rob and Ann began their roundabout journey through China and by air on to Bangkok, Yangon and Myitkyina. David, Dava and the team left Bangkok for Yangon and then caught a connection to Myitkyina. The Kachin students faced the real problems, with a long and difficult journey through the checkpoints. The Burmese army held Myitkyina, but the surrounding countryside was disputed with the KIA. Scrutiny of documents at the checkpoints was inevitable. The students could be turned around or, worse, detained at any point. This would be especially harrowing for our young men in the KIA. The planning was meticulous. To minimise suspicion, Khun Seng had arranged for the students to travel by car in small groups. They would leave at staggered times so it would not look like some kind of convoy, which would prompt investigation and searching questions. Drivers not known to the military were carefully chosen. An indirect route was taken through Bhamo and on to Myitkyina. Skirmishes on the roads had been reported but it was deemed to be the safest route. Rob and Ann arrived as scheduled and, despite the anxiety of the journey, thirty-one Kachin students drove cheerfully into Myitkyina, and David and Dava, with the precious papers bound securely, flew in from Bangkok. The following day the Cambridge exams were delivered without incident. David, who had missed his mother-in-law's funeral to complete the project, was asked if, all things considered, he was glad he'd come. He replied, "It's been brilliant, and I wouldn't have missed it for the world;" a sentiment echoed by us all. Captain Jack's theatrical exploits paled in comparison. We hoped the Cambridge admin officer had completed his course of counselling successfully and made a full recovery.

Sitting at home in the cold of an English February, we could not believe that this had been achieved. The whole project seemed, in the purest sense of the word, incredible: the young soldiers in their bunkers on the Laiza road, the bloody offensive, the flight of IDPs, the loss of so many young people, the evacuation of Rob and Ann. And through it all, the astonishing human spirit: the cheerfulness and resilience of the Kachin students, the stubborn commitment of our team, and the unflinching support of David, Dava and their colleagues. Looking at the gap on the wall where my prized sword should have been hanging, I wanted to be magnanimous and say its absence no longer seemed to matter but my 'inner John Wayne' with its gravelly whisper of 'The hell it did!' betrayed my true emotions. Nevertheless, in a strange way, Gideon had again prevailed against the odds, and that, for the moment, would be enough.

Eleven months later.

On Monday 22 January 2018 at the Grand Connaught Rooms in London, a million miles and a world away from the dusty refugee camps of the Thai border and the trenches of Kachin State, feeling quite splendid in a dinner jacket, I was with a team from Harrow International School, Bangkok, to see them win the British International Schools Outstanding Community Initiative Award for their work with MEP. There were entrants from over thirty countries, making, for International Schools, ours the best project of its type in the world. After all we had been through this was a remarkable moment. For Harrow, the award recognised its compassion, empathy and leadership. For MEP it was a vindication of the work we had done for over twenty years. We had built an organisation, been involved in the training of around two thousand teachers, taken over five hundred candidates through Cambridge exams and produced materials used by many thousands of children. We now looked to the future.

On 7 November 2020 democratic forces under Aung San Suu Kyi – The Lady who has featured many times in this narrative and who in 1996 was an inspiration for our work – won a landslide victory at the general election and planned major reforms leading to the establishment of a federal state. MEP looked to expand our programme once the threat of COVID had subsided. This was all rather premature...

Epilogue

On 1 February 2021 tanks appeared on the streets of Yangon. In a coup, the military regained control of the country and enforced martial law. Aung San Suu Kyi and her staff were arrested. Thousands took to the streets in protest. By 19 April over seven hundred people had been killed and thousands arrested.

Today, at seventy-five, Aung San Suu Kyi faces trial on some trumped-up charge. The country is locked down with all internet access cut. The notorious 33rd Light Infantry Division, active against the Rohingya and the Kachin, has been deployed to quell the protests. Fear has returned to the streets. The army behaves like an occupying force with its own people as the enemy. In response, the Karen, the Kachin and other groups have taken up arms. Air strikes by junta forces have sent thousands fleeing to the Thai border. Recent figures indicate that 250,000 people have been displaced. Full-scale civil war is a distinct possibility.

And so, a year after starting this memoir, I look at the figure of the Law Ka Nat, the one who hears the cries of the world, as it sits on my desk, motionless but charged with emotion. The cries of rage, frustration and pain are countless as Burma falls over the edge into turmoil. The democratic transition from military to civilian rule has come to naught. It was little more than a sham. Democracy was an illusion, an alluring political mirage. Nothing was as it seemed to be. The military may never have had any intention of relinquishing power, and, when its hold was threatened, reacted with brutal force. All actions have consequences, and karmic forces are building, which in the coming year could result in outcomes both dire and desirable. Despite the growing tragedy, Shiva's unending cosmic dance will inevitably continue, bringing change and, with it, hope.

Postscript

Twenty years and a lifetime ago, a voice asked, out of the darkness, "Is there anything you need, sir?" The actions and events described in this memoir stand in part as an attempt to answer that question. They were born out of a sense of adventure, a sense of history and genuine concern for what I saw. I was fascinated by all aspects of the world I had entered from its politics to its religion and languages; and this involvement enriched my life enormously and informed my own spiritual path. The journey was not undertaken alone and it didn't come without its costs. But it was a journey rather than a destination; a journey we must all undertake with compassion based not on sentimentality, but on a sense of our shared humanity tempered with a clear sense of the world as it is. And maybe this journey is the best we can ask for as human beings. Our needs run deep. Looking for something to believe in is the quest of the human heart. The desire to give oneself into helping others can come from the purity of the heart and at the same time can purify the heart. This desire may even lead some of us to follow causes and believe in '-isms'. Handled wisely this involvement can give our lives meaning and purpose, and be of benefit. However, although our intentions may be honourable, without care we can become lost in 'the haze' created by our own fears, greed and delusions of the ego. In the final count, our human journey is the quest of the herdsman mentioned in the Prologue, a spiritual journey towards an 'ancient city on an ancient hill', the wholeness of the human heart itself. I am fortunate to have travelled in such good company.

Bob Anderson
23 April 2021
Hett, Durham, England

Taking Stock

For Those Who Wish to Go Down This Path

The Bard definitely has a point; things are often not what they appear to be!

You will eventually find your Grail. Be sure to identify it.

Remember: don't be discouraged by cynics. You can't change the world; just do your best and add your light to the sum of light. But make sure you know what your light is and why it's burning.

You have only just begun. All life is transitory so there will be a time to move on. New challenges will come your way. Go back to the beginning and follow the path.

And don't sing…

Appendix

MEP Teacher-Training Model

1. Recruitment of a mobile unit of trainers. Mae La camp is divided into three zones: A, B and C. Each has about eight schools. We allocated a trainer to each zone, and one as team leader. We then found out where the schools are, identified their principal English teachers and arranged a fixed time once a week for training. We had a two-hour slot every Friday afternoon when the trainers brought together the group of teachers for training with the new materials.
2. Follow-up is crucial, so in the week following the training every trainer visited each of the schools in their cluster.
3. Telling teachers what to do is not enough. To convince them that the new techniques and materials are worthwhile you have to show them working with a class of youngsters. So, our trainers demoed new techniques and materials and taught alongside the local teachers.
4. Recruitment of a materials writer. We allocated a team

member to assess materials, identify difficulties and design new bespoke materials over an extended period for Grades 1–6.

5. Design of a system of training, and of piloting and editing materials. Grade 1 was piloted in two carefully chosen schools, ensuring continuous feedback. While Grade 1 was being piloted, Grade 2 was being written. When the final draft of Grade 1 was completed, Grade 2 was piloted while Grade 3 was written... and so on. This is a very thorough approach and pays dividends as you gradually adapt materials to local needs.

6. Ensuring sustainability in the training system allows for a turnover of teachers. We established an advanced skills teacher (AST) system based on the English model. The ASTs train incoming teachers.

Ideally, you finish up with tried-and-tested custom-made materials and a local team of trainers who are comfortable with the materials and can carry on the work. Remember, immense patience is needed to work with teachers who are accustomed only to repetition and rote learning. Confidence is built slowly. You need to select your training team carefully.

Acronyms

AMI	Aide Médicale Internationale
AST	Advanced Skills Teacher
BMWEC	Burmese Migrant Workers Education Committee
DKBA	Democratic Karen Buddhist Army
DUCK	Durham University Charities Kommittee
IDP	Internally Displaced People
KIA	Kachin Independence Army
KIO	Kachin Independence Organisation
KNLA	Karen National Liberation Army
KNU	Karen National Union
MEP	Mobile Education Partnerships (previous names KEP – Karen Education Partnership and BEP – Burma Education Partnership)
MNEC	Mon National Education Committee
NGO	Non-Governmental Organisation
NLD	National League for Democracy
NMSP	New Mon State Party
NUM	National Union of Mineworkers
PTMJC	Pu Taw Memorial Junior College
SLORC	State Law and Order Restoration Council
SOE	Special Operations Executive
USDA	Union Solidarity and Development Association
ZOA	Zuidoost Azie Refugee Care

Acknowledgements

I would like to acknowledge the role played in building this organisation by those people, often not formally involved with the charity and often outside of this narrative, who have made a significant and valuable contribution.

The staff, students and parents of Harrow International School, Bangkok. In particular the leadership of Mick Farley and Tim Jefferis, the enterprise and energy of Brian Van Den Berg and the expertise and endless goodwill of David Eastgate and Dava Romyanond and the teams of examiners who returned year after year to support our work.

Therameu Khu Paw and the staff and students of Pu Taw Memorial Junior College, Mae La Karen Refugee Camp for their example of grace, fortitude and humanity under such difficult circumstances.

The delightful students from Durham University who make up Durham University Charities Kommittee (DUCK) for their remarkable efforts at fundraising for us on cold dark nights in the North of England, for becoming our interns in

Thailand and the UK and for even delivering short courses for us in the migrant community.

Isabel Barrass, for her great generosity which has helped to build this organisation.

Phil Towns for his generosity of spirit and endless good will.

Graham and Harriet Mortimer for their wise council, kindness and friendship over the years.

Paul and Roz Sztumpf for advice, goodwill and regular support.

Greg Antos, Patrick Kearns, Fred Ligon, Simon Purnell and Scott O'Brien for their friendship and support for MEP in Thailand and Burma.

San Yu Wai Maung for her patience in teaching me the Burmese language and who, along with U Win Maung, provided much advice on all things Burmese and introduced me to a very different world.

Ian Gethin and the staff of that remarkable organisation, the FORE, who provided us with advice and the funding to bring in the valuable expertise of Julie Anne Smith.

Metinit Thongthainan (Phu) and Dan Pedersen for their friendship and innumerable kindnesses to our teams in Thailand.

Our Great North Runners especially returnees such as Jonathan Brookes, Jonny Catto, Frances Foley and Will Millard and who spend so much time training and fundraising through this remarkable event.

With particular acknowledgement to:

Will Millard, our patron, whose belief in our work, and personal example have been such an inspiration to us all.

And special remembrance of:

Hugh Corey
&
George McNeil

for the legacies they left to us without which we would never have survived or grown.

Finally, the late Chris Anderson of Durham University for his friendship and support.